444 SURPRISING
QUOTES
about the
BIBLE

A Treasury of Inspiring Thoughts & Classic Quotations

Dr. ISABELLA D. BUNN is both an international lawyer and a theologian specializing in Christian social ethics. She serves as Associate Director of the Center for Christianity and Culture at Regent's Park College, Oxford University. Isabella collaborates with her husband, novelist T. Davis Bunn, on a variety of writing projects. Having spent years rummaging around antiquarian bookstores and academic libraries, Isabella is pleased to share some of the compelling thoughts that have captured her mind and imagination.

444 SURPRISING QUOTES about the BIBLE

A Treasury of Inspiring Thoughts & Classic Quotations

COMPILED BY

Isabella D. Bunn

BETHANY HOUSE PUBLISHERS

Minneapolis, Minnesota

Published by Bethany House Publishers
11400 Hampshire Avenue South
Bloomington, Minnesota 55438

Bethany House Publishers is a division of
Baker Publishing Group, Grand Rapids, Michigan.

Printed in the United States of America

Library of Congress Cataloging-in-Publication Data

444 surprising quotes about the Bible : a treasury of inspiring thoughts and classic quotations / [compiled] by Isabella D. Bunn.
    p. cm.
    Summary: "This collection of quotations about the Scriptures from throughout history reveals the power of the Bible to transform the world"—Provided by publisher.
    Includes bibliographical references and index.
    ISBN 0-7642-0069-0 (pbk.)
    1. Bible—Miscellanea. 2. Bible—Quotations. 3. Bible—Appreciation.
I. Bunn, Isabella.
  BS538.A15   2005
  220—dc22   2005005869

CONTENTS

PREFACE

The Bible is often called the "Book of books" due to its unique standing in history, religion, and literature. It is also, quite literally, a Book of books in that it encompasses sixty-six distinct works written by scores of authors over a span of centuries. The Bible contains remarkable examples of prose and poetry, of oratories and admonitions, of songs and celebrations, of narratives and genealogies, of insights and instructions, of prophesies and parables and prayers. Indeed, the Bible can be seen as an entire library rather than just a single book—a library that is both ancient and yet continually new.

My first serious engagement with Scripture began some dozen years ago while studying theology at Oxford University. I quickly felt overwhelmed by the complexity of the Bible and the breadth of biblical scholarship. But the transforming power of the Word of God, as expressed by various writers over the ages, made a deep impression on me. I started to collect some of these observations in a file that I labeled *Words on the Word*.

My *Words on the Word* file prompted me to reflect on dimensions of Scripture that go beyond the printed page. The Word can be understood as Christ—the expression of God—the eternal

Logos instilling order in the universe. In another sense, the Word is also our appropriation of that truth by making it our own here and now. The file gradually became filled with clippings and scribblings and excerpts about the Word of God—quotations that tended to uplift, challenge, inspire, amuse, comfort, instruct, or otherwise provoke a reaction.

With time this file began to take shape as a book, expanding to cover a diverse range of themes and materials. And the publishers gave it a zingy title. From these origins, it is clear that my selection process has been more random than systematic. I did not set out to compile a volume on the most important thoughts of the most important people. Often a quote presents an especially well-turned phrase. Some crystallize a complex idea or hold a singular beauty of expression. Some are notable due to their history. Others are significant due to their source. I have included dates and designations, as indeed, it does matter whether the attribution is to a medieval mystic or a modern-day movie mogul.

All of us have experienced that slight "catching" to our breath upon beholding an especially splendid sight. This perhaps best explains my selection criteria: which ideas have caught my mind or heart or soul? My hope is that this "treasury of inspiring thoughts and classic quotations" about the Bible imparts the same feeling in the reader. And that it invites us to delve again into the Book of books, fathoming our own response.

$\mathcal{A}$CKNOWLEDGMENTS

I wish to thank my friends and colleagues at Oxford University, especially at Regent's Park College and the Centre for Christianity and Culture. Their formidable intellects, imaginations, and love of God leave me both humbled and inspired.

For their early encouragement of this book, a note of appreciation to Janet Thoma and Shannon Hill. Through their creativity and dedication, many aspiring writers have become published authors.

I am enormously grateful to Bethany House Publishers, and especially to Gary Johnson and Carol Johnson, who are true leaders and mentors in the publishing industry. Our friendship enriches me in countless ways. My editorial team at Bethany House, notably Kyle Duncan and Julie Smith, is graced with a rare combination of grand vision and attentiveness to details. They aim to serve the kingdom of God through good books, but are careful to select the right typeface for the job. I also appreciate Steve Oates, the resident marketing genius, for his valuable insights on the ever-changing world of commercial publishing.

My greatest expression of gratitude must be bestowed upon my husband, Davis. He has offered support through every stage of this project, and has patiently endured being interrupted at all hours to hear yet another quotable gem. I was deeply touched when he chose to read my first draft of the manuscript, not with the eyes of a professional author, but with the openness of a spiritual seeker. More important, it was Davis who presented me with my first Bible. Inscribing it as a Christmas gift in the early days of our courtship, he wrote: "For Isabella, On the occasion of our growing love for God and for one another." And *that* is the single most life-transforming quotation about the Bible I have ever encountered.

The POWER of the BIBLE to
ENCOURAGE FAITH

*F*or the word of God is living and active. Sharper than any double-edged sword, it penetrates even to dividing soul and spirit, joints and marrow; it judges the thoughts and attitudes of the heart. . . .

Therefore, since we have a great high priest who has gone through the heavens, Jesus the Son of God, let us hold firmly to the faith we possess.

HEBREWS 4:12, 14

Never approach the words of the mysteries that are in the Scriptures without praying and asking for God's help. Say, "Lord grant me to feel the power that is in them." Reckon prayer to be the key that opens the true meaning of Scriptures.

ISAAC OF NINEVEH (SEVENTH CENTURY)
SYRIAN SPIRITUAL WRITER

The Scripture was written that we might know what to hope for from God.

MATTHEW HENRY (1662–1714)
ENGLISH BIBLE COMMENTATOR

It is less important to ask a Christian what he or she believes about the Bible than to inquire what he or she does with it.

LESSLIE NEWBIGIN (1905–1998)
BRITISH REFORMED THEOLOGIAN, MISSIONARY AND
ECUMENICAL LEADER

Walking in faith brings you to the Word of God. There you will be healed, cleansed, fed, nurtured, equipped, and matured.

KAY ARTHUR
AUTHOR AND FOUNDER OF PRECEPT MINISTRIES
INTERNATIONAL

The Bible without the Holy Spirit is a sundial by moonlight.

DWIGHT L. MOODY (1837–1899)
AMERICAN EVANGELIST AND FOUNDER OF BIBLE INSTITUTE

The Bible, like other classics of religion and literature, does not disclose its meaning without interpretation. . . . . For Christians, however, the Bible is also sacred Scripture. It is a holy book whose history narrates the story of salvation and whose teaching imparts divine wisdom.

ROBERT L. WILKEN
PROFESSOR OF CHRISTIAN HISTORY
HARPER'S BIBLE COMMENTARY, 1988

The vigour of our spiritual life will be in exact proportion to the place held by the Bible in our life and thoughts.

GEORGE MUELLER (1805–1898)
PRUSSIAN MEMBER OF THE OPEN BRETHREN

The Bible has its own special and irreplaceable role in the history of redemption. We can refer any person to it with the assurance that if they will approach it openly, honestly, intelligently and persistently, God will meet them through its pages and speak peace to their souls.

DALLAS WILLARD
SOUTHERN BAPTIST MINISTER, THEOLOGIAN AND SCHOLAR
HEARING GOD, 1999

Therefore the Scriptures should only be read in an attitude of prayer, trusting the inward working of the Holy Spirit to make their truths a living reality within us.

WILLIAM LAW (1686–1761)
ENGLISH CONTEMPLATIVE AND CLERIC
THE POWER OF THE SPIRIT, 1761

Scripture functions toward sanctification.

BREVARD S. CHILDS
PROFESSOR OF DIVINITY AT YALE UNIVERSITY
BIBLICAL THEOLOGY OF THE OLD & NEW TESTAMENTS, 1993

As I spent time chewing over the endless assurances and promises to be found in the Bible, so my faith in the living God grew stronger and held me safe in his hands. God's word to us, especially his word spoken by his spirit through the Bible, is the very ingredient that feeds our faith. If we feed our souls regularly on God's word, several times each day, we should become robust spiritually just as we feed on ordinary food several times each day and become robust physically. Nothing is more important than hearing and obeying the word of God.

DAVID WATSON
FEAR NO EVIL: A PERSONAL STRUGGLE WITH CANCER, 1984

So the Bible is primarily a book neither of science, nor of literature, nor of philosophy, but of salvation. In saying this we must give the word "salvation" its broadest possible meaning. Salvation is far more than merely the forgiveness of sins. It includes the whole sweep of God's purpose to redeem and restore humankind, and indeed all creation. What we claim for the Bible is that it unfolds God's total plan.

JOHN R. W. STOTT
RECTOR EMERITUS OF ALL SOULS CHURCH, LONDON
UNDERSTANDING THE BIBLE, 2001

Through reading the Word, I learned that God does want to talk to us and that He has a plan for our lives that will lead us to a place of peace and contentment.

JOYCE MEYER
INSPIRATIONAL AUTHOR AND BROADCASTER
HOW TO HEAR FROM GOD, 2003

It outlives, out lifts, outloves, outreaches, outranks, outruns all other books.
Trust it, love it, obey it, and Eternal life is yours.

A. Z. CONRAD
AMERICAN PASTOR AND EVANGELIST
(ON THE QUALITIES OF THE BIBLE)

The Holy Scriptures are our letters from home.

ST. AUGUSTINE OF HIPPO (354-430)
DOCTOR OF THE CHURCH AND PHILOSOPHER

I did not go through the book. The book went
through me.

A. W. TOZER (AIDEN WILSON TOZER) (1897-1963)
AMERICAN PASTOR AND WRITER

Words fail to express my love for this holy Book, my
gratitude for its author, for His love and goodness.
How shall I thank Him for it?

LOTTIE MOON (1840-1912)
AMERICAN MISSIONARY TO CHINA

The apostles at that time first preached the Gospel
but later, by the will of God, they delivered it to us
in the Scriptures, that it might be the foundation
and pillar of our faith.

ST. JEROME (C.342-420)
DALMATIAN-BORN CHURCH FATHER
(TRANSLATOR OF ORIGINAL-LANGUAGE TEXTS INTO THE
LATIN BIBLE VERSION KNOWN AS *THE VULGATE*)

Cultivate your spiritual memory; live in your remembrances of faith. . . . Never let Jesus' words be wasted upon you and your experience evaporate and be found no more.

JOSEPH PARKER (1830-1902)
ENGLISH CONGREGATIONALIST PREACHER AND
BIBLE COMMENTATOR

I felt myself absolutely born again. The gates of Paradise had been flung open and I had entered. There and then the whole of scripture took on another look to me.

MARTIN LUTHER (1485-1546)
GERMAN MONK, THEOLOGIAN AND LEADER OF THE
PROTESTANT REFORMATION

I prayed for Faith, and thought that some day Faith would come down and strike me like lightning. But Faith did not seem to come. One day I read in the tenth chapter of Romans, "Now Faith cometh by hearing, and hearing by the Word of God." I had closed my Bible, and prayed for Faith. I now opened my Bible, and began to study, and Faith has been growing ever since.

DWIGHT L. MOODY (1837-1899)
AMERICAN EVANGELIST AND FOUNDER OF BIBLE INSTITUTE

Little of the Word with little prayer is death to the spiritual life. Much of the Word with little prayer gives a sickly life. Much prayer with little of the Word gives more life, but without steadfastness. A full measure of the Word and prayer each day gives a healthy and powerful life.

ANDREW MURRAY (1828-1917)
PREACHER AND AUTHOR IN SOUTH AFRICA AND SCOTLAND
THE PRAYER LIFE

The Bible, then, has an essential place in the life of a Christian. For the revelation of God leads to worship, the warnings of God to repentance, the promises of God to faith, the commands of God to obedience and the truth of God to witness. It is no exaggeration to say that without Scripture a Christian life is impossible.

JOHN R. W. STOTT
RECTOR EMERITUS OF ALL SOULS CHURCH, LONDON
UNDERSTANDING THE BIBLE, 2001

The sacred books are pervaded by the Spirit. There is nothing either in the prophets, or in the law, or in the Gospels, or in the epistles, which does not spring from the fullness of the divine majesty.

ORIGEN (C.185-254)
ALEXANDRIAN BIBLICAL SCHOLAR AND SPIRITUAL WRITER

The wise man has got to know his God. That is the
goal of all our Bible study!

STEPHEN MOTYER
UNLOCK THE BIBLE, 1990

If you knew the whole Bible by heart and all the
teachings of the philosophers, how would this help
you without the grace and love of God?

THOMAS À KEMPIS (C.1380–1471)
GERMAN MONK, MYSTIC AND WRITER
THE IMITATION OF CHRIST

You can only understand Scripture on your knees.

MAURICE ZUNDEL (1897–1975)
SWISS PRIEST, POET AND THEOLOGIAN

The Bible is not an end in itself, but a means to bring
men to an intimate and satisfying knowledge of God,
that they may enter into Him, that they may delight
in His Presence, may taste and know the inner
sweetness of the very God Himself in the core and
center of their hearts.

A. W. TOZER (AIDEN WILSON TOZER) (1897–1963)
AMERICAN PASTOR AND WRITER
THE PURSUIT OF GOD, 1948

To see in the Bible nothing more than a collection of ordinary human contributions to religious literature would be, in the judgment of those who know it best and prize it most, to fail to see in it that which is its highest and most noble characteristic, namely, a message of God to the human soul—a message of highest moral and spiritual value not to the people of past ages only but to all generations of men in all ages.

WILBUR F. TILLETT
THE ABINGDON BIBLE COMMENTARY, 1929

The Bible, of course, knows nothing of the Enlightenment; but it has a good deal to say about what happens when the human race believes that its destiny is best left to humanity.

THE OXFORD ILLUSTRATED HISTORY OF THE BIBLE, 2001

The "heart" in the biblical sense is not the inward life, but the whole man in relation to God.

DIETRICH BONHOEFFER (1905-1945)
GERMAN THEOLOGIAN
(IMPRISONED AND EXECUTED BY THE NAZIS)

The way to understand the Scriptures and all theology is to become holy. It is to be under the authority of the Spirit.

DAVID MARTYN LLOYD-JONES (1899-1981)
WELSH PREACHER AND WRITER

This is the secret of the Psalms. Our identity is hidden in them. In them we find ourselves and God. In these fragments he has revealed not only himself to us but ourselves to him.

THOMAS MERTON (1915-1968)
FRENCH-BORN TRAPPIST MONK AND POET

This Book has the power not only to inform—but to reform and to transform lives. . . . It is supernatural in origin, eternal in duration, divine in authorship, infallible in authority, inexhaustible in meaning, universal in readership, unique in revelation, personal in application and powerful in effect. . . . Come to it with awe, read it with reverence, frequently, slowly, prayerfully.

THE GIDEONS INTERNATIONAL
(PREFACE TO THE BIBLE)

The holy Scriptures are that divine instrument by which we are taught what to believe, concerning God, ourselves, and all things, and how to please God unto eternal life.

JOHN ROBINSON (1919-1983)
ENGLISH THEOLOGIAN AND BISHOP OF WOOLWICH

Translation it is that openeth the window, to let in the light; that breaketh the shell, that we may eat the kernel; that putteth aside the curtain, that we may look into the most Holy place; that removeth the cover of the well, that we may come by the water. . . .

THE HOLY BIBLE *KING JAMES VERSION*
(*THE AUTHORIZED VERSION*), 1611
(MESSAGE FROM THE TRANSLATORS TO THE READER)

Thought should be given to the more extensive use of the Word of God. . . . The more at home the Word of God is among us, the more we shall bring about faith and its fruits.

PHILIPP JAKOB SPENER (1635-1705)
GERMAN LUTHER PASTOR AND FOUNDER OF PIETISM
PIOUS LONGINGS, 1675

Pay attention to the reading of the words of
Scripture, in order to learn from them how
to be with God.

JOHN OF APAMEA (EARLY FIFTH CENTURY)
SYRIAN MONK AND SPIRITUAL WRITER

How firm a foundation, Ye saints of the Lord,
Is laid for your faith in His excellent Word!
What more can He say than to you He hath said,
To you who for refuge to Jesus have fled?

ATTRIBUTED TO ''K''
RIPPON'S *SELECTION OF HYMNS*, 1787
''HOW FIRM A FOUNDATION''

These books have been loved because of their
inspired linguistic perfection. Treasured words
encourage, console and save.

IRIS MURDOCH (1919-1999)
ENGLISH MORAL PHILOSOPHER AND NOVELIST
(ON *THE* HOLY BIBLE *KING JAMES VERSION* AND *THE BOOK OF
COMMON PRAYER*)

He who hath heard the Word of God
can bear his silences.

ST. IGNATIUS OF LOYOLA (1491-1556)
SPANISH THEOLOGIAN AND FOUNDER OF THE JESUIT ORDER

The words of God which you receive by your ear,
hold fast in your heart. For the Word of God is the
food of the soul.

ST. GREGORY THE GREAT (540-604)
POPE, CHURCH FATHER AND TEACHER

Our primary task is to create the space for the word
of God to once again cut into our daily life
experience, in order to redeem and liberate it.

THOMAS CULLINAN
BENEDICTINE MONK AND SOCIAL ACTIVIST

Our reading of the gospel story can be and should be
an act of personal communion with
the living Lord.

WILLIAM TEMPLE (1881-1944)
BRITISH CLERGYMAN

According to the Scriptures the Spirit is the first
and principal leader.

ROBERT BARCLAY (1648-1690)
SCOTTISH QUAKER

. . . suddenly from a house close by, I heard the voice
of a boy or girl, I don't know which, singing and
constantly repeating the words: "Take and read.

Take and read."
... Stifling my tears I rose, reckoning that this was
nothing less than a command from God to open the
book and read the first passage I came upon. I went
back to the place where I had put down the book of
St. Paul's Epistles ... I seized it and read in silence
the first passage my eyes fell upon. ... I had no
wish to read further, and there was no need. The
moment I came to the end of this sentence, the light
of certainty flooded my heart, as it were, and every
cloud of hesitation rolled away.

ST. AUGUSTINE OF HIPPO (354-430)
DOCTOR OF THE CHURCH AND PHILOSOPHER
CONFESSIONS

Lay hold on the Bible until the Bible
lays hold on you.

WILLIAM H. HOUGHTON
PRESIDENT OF THE MOODY BIBLE INSTITUTE, 1934-1947

There is a living God. He has spoken in the Bible.
He means what he says and will do all
he has promised.

JAMES HUDSON TAYLOR (1832-1905)
ENGLISH MEDICAL MISSIONARY

Responsive listening is the form the Bible gives to our basic religious quest as human beings.

DAVID STEINDL-RAST
AUSTRIAN BENEDICTINE MONK AND SPIRITUAL WRITER

The Word of God gives us great help in attaining the peace we need. It is living, very lively and active in seizing the conscience of the sinner, in cutting him to the heart, and in comforting him and binding up the wounds of the soul. It is powerful. It convinces powerfully, converts powerfully, and comforts powerfully.

MATTHEW HENRY (1662–1714)
ENGLISH BIBLE COMMENTATOR

Through meditating on the Word we witness and are witnessed, and are brought to the experience of all that "is said, and done, and doing" in ourselves. The Word of God is active, informing both the beginner's first uncertain prayer and the contemplative's silent rapture.

LORRAINE KISLY
WATCH AND PRAY: CHRISTIAN TEACHINGS ON THE
PRACTICE OF PRAYER, 2002

For in the sacred books, the Father who is in heaven
meets His children with great love and speaks with
them; and the force and power in the word of God is
so great that it remains the support and energy of the
Church, the strength and faith of her children, the
food of the soul, the pure and perennial source
of spiritual life.

WILLIAM JOHNSTON
CHRISTIAN MYSTICISM TODAY, 1998

We are to hear. All of us are. That is what the whole
Bible is calling out. "Hear, O Israel!" But hear what?
Hear what? The Bible is hundreds upon hundreds of
voices all calling out at once out of the past and
clamoring for our attention. . . . And somewhere in
the midst of them all one particular voice speaks out
that is unlike any other voice because it speaks so
directly to the deepest privacy and longing and
weariness of each of us that there are times when the
centuries are blown away like mist, and it is as if we
stand with no shelter of time at all between ourselves
and the one who speaks our secret name. Come, the
voice says. Unto me. All ye. Every last one.

FREDERICK BUECHNER
AWARD-WINNING AUTHOR AND CHRISTIAN APOLOGIST
A ROOM CALLED REMEMBER, 1984

When you shall see a soul which, having left all, cleaves unto the Word with every thought and desire; lives only for the Word, rules itself according to the Word and becomes fruitful by the Word—which is able to say with St. Paul, "for me to live is Christ and to die is gain"—then you may have assurance that this soul is a bride wedded to the Word.

BERNARD OF CLAIRVAUX (1091–1153)
FRENCH MONK AND FOUNDER OF THE CISTERIAN ORDER
SERMON ON THE SONG OF SONGS

I am a man of one book.

ST. THOMAS AQUINAS (1225–74)
ITALIAN DOMINICAN FRIAR, THEOLOGIAN AND DOCTOR OF
THE CHURCH

Pray and read, read and pray; for a little from God is better than a great deal from men.

JOHN BUNYAN (1628–1688)
ENGLISH WRITER AND NONCONFORMIST PREACHER

Some persons when they hear of the prayer of quiet falsely imagine that the soul remains stupid, dead and inactive. But unquestionably it acts therein, more nobly and more extensively than it had ever done before, for God himself is the mover and the soul now acts by the agency of his Spirit . . . Our activity

should, therefore, consist in endeavoring to acquire
and maintain such a state as may be most susceptible
of divine impressions, most flexile to all the
operations of the Eternal Word.

MADAME GUYON (JEANNE-MARIE BOUVIER GUYON)
(1648-1717)
FRENCH MYSTIC
A SHORT AND VERY EASY METHOD OF PRAYER, 1685

The heart of man was made to receive the Word, and
the Word adapts itself to the dimensions
of the human heart.

ANDRÉ LOUF
FRENCH CISTERCIAN ABBOTT
TEACH US TO PRAY, 1992

Anyone entering the sphere of radiance of the divine
word is held fast by it; he knows from experience
that this word not only communicates knowledge
about God, but—hidden within the garb of the letter—
actually has divine qualities; in itself it is an
overpowering manifestation of God's infinity and
truth, his majesty and love.

HANS URS VON BALTHASAR (1905-1988)
SWISS ROMAN CATHOLIC THEOLOGIAN
PRAYER, 1986

I picked up my Bible and read verse 10 [of
1 Chronicles 4]—the prayer of Jabez. Something in his
prayer would explain the mystery. It had to. Pulling a
chair up to the yellow counter, I bent over my Bible,
and reading the prayer over and over, I searched
with all my heart for the future God had for someone
as ordinary as I.
The next morning, I prayed Jabez's prayer
word for word.
And the next.
And the next.
Thirty years later, I haven't stopped.

BRUCE WILKERSON
FOUNDER OF WALK THRU THE BIBLE MINISTRIES
THE PRAYER OF JABEZ, 2000

But it is especially the *Gospels* which sustain me
during my hours of prayer, for in them I find what is
necessary for my poor little soul. I am constantly
discovering in them new lights, hidden and
mysterious meanings.

ST. THÉRÈSE OF LISIEUX (1873–1897)
FRENCH CARMELITE NUN
STORY OF A SOUL

read. think. pray. live.
When God's Word starts to come alive in your life,
you can't help but pray—
here, there, everywhere. *Pray all the time.* Lose
yourself in God's Word.

CHRISTIANITY TODAY, FEBRUARY 2004
(ADVERTISEMENT FOR *THE MESSAGE: THE BIBLE IN
CONTEMPORARY LANGUAGE*)

What comes out of the bulk of the biblical references
to the soul seems to be this: there is a special part of
us that reflects and draws us toward what is
uniquely us in potential. This part focuses our most
important spiritual and ethical awareness, and deals
with our search for God and with evaluating the
reality around us, urging us to integrate with
integrity that which appears to be God's will for our
lives. Biblical and secular writers seem to agree that
without integrity there is ultimately no spiritual
journey. Honesty is not the best policy for the soul;
it's the only policy.

J. KEITH MILLER
THE SECRET LIFE OF THE SOUL, 1999

We are mistaken when we look at the Bible as a spiritual toolbox. We can't take things out of the Bible and make them work for us. The whole process of the spiritual life is to come before the God who is alive, who becomes present to us in his Word, and who by means of that Word creates and redeems us. We don't use Scripture; God uses Scripture to work his will in us.

EUGENE H. PETERSON
PRESBYTERIAN CHURCH PASTOR AND WRITER

God is pleased to use Scripture to pierce the heart and awaken us to faith. . . . History is replete with stories of how great people were converted through the power of the Word.

R. C. SPROUL
PROFESSOR OF THEOLOGY AND CHAIRMAN OF LIGONIER
MINISTRIES
FIVE THINGS EVERY CHRISTIAN NEEDS TO GROW, 2002

The Word of God is in the Bible like the soul is in the body.

PETER TAYLOR FORSYTH (1848–1921)
CONGREGATIONALIST PASTOR AND THEOLOGIAN

The history of all the great characters of the Bible is summed up in this one sentence: They acquainted themselves with God, and acquiesced in His will in all things.

RICHARD CECIL (1748–1810)
ANGLICAN PREACHER

Holy Scripture containeth all things necessary to salvation.

ARTICLES OF RELIGION
THE BOOK OF COMMON PRAYER, 1562

Christianity is different from all other religions. They are the story of man's search for God. The Gospel is the story of God's search for man.

DEWI MORGAN
RECTOR OF ST. BRIDE'S, LONDON
ST. MARY'S MESSENGER, SEPTEMBER 1966

It gives me a deep comforting sense that "things seen are temporal and things unseen are eternal."

HELEN KELLER (1880–1968)
AMERICAN WRITER AND SOCIAL REFORMER
(BLIND AND DEAF FROM THE AGE OF 19 MONTHS; ON
READING THE BIBLE DAILY, 1955)

But among all our joys, there was no one that more filled our hearts, than the blessed continuance of the preaching of God's sacred Word among us; which is that inestimable treasure, which excelleth all the riches of the earth; because the fruit thereof extendeth itself, not only to the time spent in this transitory world, but directeth and disposeth men to that eternal happiness which is above in heaven.

THE HOLY BIBLE *KING JAMES VERSION (THE AUTHORIZED VERSION)*, 1611
(MESSAGE OF DEDICATION FROM THE TRANSLATORS TO THE KING)

As in Paradise, God walks in Scripture, seeking man.

ST. AMBROSE (c. 339–397)
BISHOP OF MILAN AND CHURCH FATHER

———◆◆◆———

But these are written that you may believe that Jesus is the Christ, the Son of God, and that by believing you may have life in his name.

JOHN 20:31

The POWER of the BIBLE to
PROVIDE
INSTRUCTION

*B*ut as for you, continue in what you have learned and become convinced of. . . . All scripture is God-breathed and is useful for teaching, rebuking, correcting and training in righteousness, so that the man of God can be equipped for every good work.

2 TIMOTHY 3:14, 16–17

Blessed Lord, who caused all Holy Scriptures to be written for our learning: help us so to hear them, to read, mark, learn, and inwardly digest them, that, through patience and the comfort of your holy word, we may embrace and forever hold fast the hope of everlasting life, which you have given us in our Savior Jesus Christ.

COLLECT FOR ADVENT
THE ALTERNATIVE SERVICE BOOK, 1980

Just as those at sea, who have been carried away
from the direction of the harbor they are making for,
regain the right course by the clear sign of some
beacon or mountain peak, so the Scripture guides
those adrift on the sea of life back to the harbor
of God's will.

GREGORY OF NYSSA (C.335–394)
CHURCH FATHER FROM CAPPODOCIA

The secret of my success? It is simple. It is found in
the Bible, "In all thy ways acknowledge Him and
He shall direct thy paths."

GEORGE WASHINGTON CARVER (1864–1943)
AMERICAN INVENTOR AND HORTICULTURALIST

In the heart of every Christian, in the in-most depths
of each person, there is always an echo of the
question which the young man in the Gospel asked
Jesus: "Teacher, what must I do to have
eternal life?"

POPE JOHN PAUL II (1920-2005)
POLISH PRIEST AND PHILOSOPHER
ENCYCLICAL LETTER *VERITATIS SPLENDOR*, 1993

In the Bible there is enough clarity to enlighten the
Elect, and enough obscurity to humble them.

BLAISE PASCAL (1623–1662)
FRENCH PHILOSOPHER, MATHEMATICIAN AND PHYSICIST

The Bible demands commentary because of its
importance and character. It contains the sacred
Scriptures of Judaism and Christianity and the primal
literature of our culture; its significance for religion
and culture calls for perennial work to interpret its
texts in every generation. The books collected in the
Bible were written in three different languages, in a
succession of cultures, across centuries of time. To
understand them, we need to call upon all the
resources which the new knowledge available in our
time can provide about their languages,
cultures, and thought.

JAMES L. MAYS
HARPER'S BIBLE COMMENTARY, 1988

The scriptures teach us the best way of living, the
noblest way of suffering, and the most comfortable
way of dying.

JOHN FLAVEL (c.1639–1691)
ENGLISH PRESBYTERIAN MINISTER

Apply yourself wholly to the scriptures, and apply
the scriptures wholly to yourself.

JOHANNES ALBRECHT BENGEL (1687–1752)
LUTHERAN NEW TESTAMENT SCHOLAR

The centre of the gospel is not about knowledge, but
about love: the love of God for a fallen world, and his
will to restore it through Christ. About this gospel
the Bible—in both Testaments—provides us with all
kinds of information, both historical and theological.
By reading the Bible, studying it with all our critical
powers, using it in worship, and being challenged by
it as a literary text, we can come face to face with the
gospel and respond to it with our whole lives.

JOHN BARTON
PROFESSOR OF THE INTERPRETATION OF HOLY SCRIPTURE
AT OXFORD UNIVERSITY
PEOPLE OF THE BOOK? 1988

The Bible, as a revelation from God, was not
designed to give us all the information we might
desire, nor to solve all the questions about which the
human soul is perplexed, but to impart enough to be
a safe guide to the haven of eternal rest.

ALBERT BARNES (1798–1870)
AMERICAN PRESBYTERIAN PASTOR AND BIBLE COMMENTATOR

. . . I studied the Bible again to find an answer to the guiding question of my life: How does spiritual growth address and solve life's problems? . . . *I saw that everything I had been learning that helped people grow was right there in the Bible all along.* All of the processes that had changed people's lives were in the pages of Scripture. The Bible talked about the things that helped people grow in relational and emotional areas as well as spiritual ones. I was ecstatic. Not only was the Bible true, but also what was true was in the Bible!

HENRY TOWNSEND
IN JOHN CLOUD AND HENRY TOWNSEND
*HOW PEOPLE GROW: WHAT THE BIBLE REVEALS ABOUT
PERSONALITY GROWTH*, 2001

So the Bible is to help us learn how to live in the kingdom of God here and now. It teaches us how to morph. It is indispensable for this task. I have never known someone leading a spiritually transformed life who had not been deeply saturated in Scripture.

JOHN ORTBERG
TEACHING PASTOR AT WILLOW CREEK CHURCH
THE LIFE YOU'VE ALWAYS WANTED, 1997

The central conception of Man in the Gospels is that
he is an unfinished creation capable of reaching a
higher level by a definite evolution which must
begin by his own efforts.

MAURICE NICOLL (1884–1953)
SCOTTISH PHYSICIAN AND PHILOSOPHER
THE NEW MAN, 1950

The only way to understand the difficult parts of the
Bible is first to read and obey the easy ones.

JOHN RUSKIN (1819–1900)
ENGLISH ART AND SOCIAL CRITIC

. . . We come now to the question as to how God's
guidance is to come to us, and how we shall be able
to know his voice. There are four ways in which He
reveals His will to us—through the Scriptures, through
providential circumstances, through the convictions
of our own higher judgment, and through the inward
impressions of the Holy Spirit on our minds. . . .

The Scriptures come first. If you are in doubt upon
any subject, you must, first of all, consult the Bible
about it, and see whether there is any law there to
direct you. Until you have found and obeyed God's
will as it is there revealed, you must not ask nor

expect a separate, direct, personal revelation. A great many fatal mistakes are made in the matter of guidance by the overlooking of this simple rule.

HANNAH WHITALL SMITH (1832–1911)
QUAKER EVANGELIST
THE CHRISTIAN'S SECRET OF A HAPPY LIFE, 1870

The word of God tends to make large-minded, noble-hearted men.

HENRY WARD BEECHER (1813–1887)
AMERICAN CLERGYMAN AND ABOLITIONIST

Take away, O Lord, the veil of my heart while I read the scriptures.
Blessed art thou, O Lord: O Teach me thy statutes!
Give me a word, O Word of the Father: touch my heart: enlighten the understanding of my heart: open my lips and fill them with thy praise.

LANCELOT ANDREWES (1555–1626)
ENGLISH BISHOP AND PREACHER

Every Christian ought to be a Bible Reader. It is the One Habit, which, if done in the right spirit, more than any other one habit, will make a Christian what he ought to be in every way.

HALLEY'S BIBLE HANDBOOK, 1965

If there is any one fact or doctrine, or command, or promise in the Bible which has produced no practical effect on your temper, or heart, or conduct, be assured you do not truly believe it.

EDWARD PAYSON (1783–1827)
AMERICAN CONGREGATIONALIST PASTOR AND PREACHER

It's time to listen. To people and to God. There is nothing more foolish than an answer to an unasked question or a response to an unexpressed need. And there is nothing more impelling than *God's answers* in the Bible to people's most urgent questions and *his* response to their deepest needs.

LLOYD J. OGILVIE
FORMER CHAPLAIN OF THE U.S. SENATE
ASKING GOD YOUR HARDEST QUESTIONS, 2004

Bible reading is an education in itself.

LORD TENNYSON (ALFRED) (1809–1892)
ENGLISH POET

How petty are the books of the philosophers, with all their pomp, compared with the Gospels!

JEAN-JACQUES ROUSSEAU (1712–1778)
FRENCH PHILOSOPHER AND NOVELIST

Teaching that lacks grace may enter our ears but it never reaches the heart. When the grace of God really touches our inmost mind so as to bring understanding, then the word that reaches our ear can also sink deeply into the heart.

ISIDORE OF SEVILLE (C.560–636)
SPANISH ARCHBISHOP AND SCHOLAR

The Bible is a book about God the heavenly Father, the author of everything that is good and beautiful and true, and the mysterious relationship he has with his children. As such, it never wanders far from life's greatest interests and problems.

ROGER STEER
GOOD NEWS FOR THE WORLD: THE STORY OF
THE BIBLE SOCIETY, 2004

From the patristic period to the Reformation scripture was the foundation text of all intellectual endeavour. All formal education was a preparation for reading it and its study the supreme task of the most advanced scholars of the medieval universities.

THE OXFORD ILLUSTRATED HISTORY OF THE BIBLE, 2001

When you read the Bible, you are reading God's message for you. The Bible is not just an option for knowing God and the secrets of the universe. It is the *only* way to discover the details of God's plan for you. For example, through the Bible you can learn that God created you. You can discover that God loved you so much that He sent Jesus to earth so you could see what God is like in person. And you can find out that Jesus is coming back to earth again in the future.

The Bible has all of that and more. So don't waste another day. Dust off that Bible in your house and open it. As you read, God will begin to speak to you. And what He has to say may very well change your life.

BRUCE BICKEL AND STAN JANTZ
GOD IS IN THE SMALL STUFF—AND IT ALL MATTERS, 1998

The time especially appropriate for laying foundation stones . . . is the morning hour when you lecture . . . therefore all your lectures especially at that time should be on the books of the New Testament or the Old.

ROBERT GROSSETESTE (C.1168-1253)
ENGLISH BISHOP AND SCHOLAR

The Bible is the one Book to which any thoughtful
man may go with any honest question of life or
destiny and find the answer of God by
honest searching.

JOHN RUSKIN (1819-1900)
ENGLISH ART AND SOCIAL CRITIC

The Scriptures were not given to increase our
knowledge but to change our lives.

DWIGHT L. MOODY (1837-1899)
AMERICAN EVANGELIST AND FOUNDER OF BIBLE INSTITUTE

But still ye will say I can not understand it. What
marvel? How shouldest thou understand, if thou wilt
not read, nor look upon it? Take the books into thine
hands, read the whole story, and that thou
understandest, keep it well in memory; that thou
understandest not, read it again, and again. If thou
can neither so come by it, counsel with some other
that is better learned.

THOMAS CRANMER (1489-1556)
ANGLICAN ARCHBISHOP OF CANTERBURY AND MARTYR
PREFACE TO THE GREAT BIBLE, 1540

An honest man with an open Bible and a pad and pencil is sure to find out what is wrong with him very quickly.

A. W. TOZER (AIDEN WILSON TOZER) (1897–1963)
AMERICAN PASTOR AND WRITER

God has not left us in the dark to wonder and guess. He has clearly revealed his five purposes for our lives through the Bible. It is our Owner's Manual, explaining why we are alive, how life works, what to avoid, and what to expect in the future. . . . To discover your purpose in life you must turn to God's Word, not the world's wisdom.

RICK WARREN
PASTOR OF SADDLEBACK CHURCH IN CALIFORNIA
THE PURPOSE-DRIVEN LIFE, 2002

O Lord, who has given us thy Word for a light to shine upon our path: Grant us to meditate upon that Word and to follow its teaching that we may find in it the light that shineth more and more unto the perfect day; Through Jesus Christ our Lord.

ST. JEROME (C.342–420)
DALMATIAN-BORN CHURCH FATHER
(TRANSLATOR OF ORIGINAL-LANGUAGE TEXTS INTO THE
LATIN BIBLE VERSION KNOWN AS *THE VULGATE*)

Throw away thy rod,
Throw away thy wrath;
O my God,
Take the gentle path.

For my heart's desire
Unto thine is bent;
I aspire
To a full consent.

Not a word or look
I affect to own,
But by book,
And thy book alone.

GEORGE HERBERT (1593–1633)
WELSH POET AND PREACHER
"DISCIPLINE"

Let it be a law for ourselves, then, that we should
run after perfection. Once we have heard the word of
truth and of mercy, let us be "the good soil" for it,
and let it put forth in us rootlets, striking root in our
souls, and sprouting so as to "give fruit, thirty-fold,
sixty-fold and a hundred-fold."

BOOK OF STEPS
SYRIAN WRITING OF THE LATE FOURTH CENTURY

O God, open my eyes to know the task
which only I can do
and give me grace to do it.
Be it unto me according to thy word.

RICHARD HARRIES
BISHOP OF OXFORD
PRAYER AND THE PURSUIT OF HAPPINESS, 1985

The sovereign God can arrange things so as to have
us read a specific passage on the very day we most
need to hear its message. So the fact that we may
read that passage on that day may not be simply a
coincidence. It may well be an instance of
direct divine guidance.

AJITH FERNANDO
YOUTH FOR CHRIST, SRI LANKA

Pour into their untaught minds the preaching of both
the Old and New Testaments in the spirit of virtue
and love and sobriety and with reasoning suited
to their understanding.

BONIFACE (C.680-754)
ENGLISH MISSIONARY TO GERMANY

Be a proclaimer of the gospel at all times. You will become a proclaimer of the gospel when you lay upon yourself the gospel's way of life.

JOHN OF APAMEA (EARLY FIFTH CENTURY)
SYRIAN MONK AND SPIRITUAL WRITER

The study of God's Word for the purpose of discovering God's Will is the secret discipline which has formed the greatest characters.

JAMES W. ALEXANDER (1804–1859)
AMERICAN PREACHER AND THEOLOGIAN

The Holy Scriptures tell us what we could never learn any other way: they tell us what we are, who we are, how we got here, why we are here, and what we are required to do while we remain here.

A. W. TOZER (AIDEN WILSON TOZER) (1897–1963)
AMERICAN PASTOR AND WRITER

The reformation which is brought about by a coercive power will be only outward and superficial; but that which is done by God's Word will be inward and lasting.

GEORGE WHITEFIELD (1714–1770)
BRITISH EVANGELIST

This epistle is in truth the most important document in the New Testament, the gospel in its purest expression. Not only is it well worth a Christian's while to know it word for word by heart, but also to meditate on it day by day. It is the soul's daily bread, and can never be read too often, or too much.

MARTIN LUTHER (1485-1546)
GERMAN MONK, THEOLOGIAN AND LEADER OF THE
PROTESTANT REFORMATION
(ON THE LETTER TO THE ROMANS)

Obedience is all over the Gospels. The pliability of an obedient heart must be complete from the set of our wills right on through our actions.

CATHERINE MARSHALL (1914-1983)
AMERICAN RELIGIOUS WRITER AND AUTHOR OF
THE NOVEL *CHRISTY*, 1967

I do not sit down to the perusal of scripture in order to impose a sense on the inspired writers, but to receive one, as they give it me. I pretend not to teach them, I wish like a child to be taught by them.

CHARLES SIMEON (1759-1836)
ENGLISH EVANGELICAL CLERGYMAN

Theology is relative to the word of God. . . . It means that theology is occupied in continuous attentive and obedient listening to the word of God.

GERRIT C. BERKOUWER (1903–1966)
DUTCH REFORMED THEOLOGIAN

Every one has not only a right, but it is his bounden duty to read the holy Scriptures in a language which he understands, and edify himself thereby.

PHILARET OF MOSCOW (1782–1867)
RUSSIAN ORTHODOX METROPOLITAN OF MOSCOW

There are two things to do about the Gospel—believe it and behave it.

SUSANNA WESLEY (1669–1742)
MOTHER OF JOHN AND CHARLES WESLEY

The Bible should be taught so early and so thoroughly that it sinks straight to the bottom of the mind where everything that comes along can settle on it.

NORTHROP FRYE (1912–1991)
CANADIAN CHURCHMAN AND CHANCELLOR OF
VICTORIA UNIVERSITY

The Bible speaks of God's command in order to call our attention not merely to what the will and work and self-revelation were there and then, but to what they are here and now for ourselves. In its capacity as witness it claims not only our recognition of facts but also our faith, not merely our appreciation of the past events which it attests but also our realisation that matters are still the same here and now, and that as and what God commanded and forbade others, He now commands and forbids us.

KARL BARTH (1886–1968)
SWISS REFORMED THEOLOGIAN
CHURCH DOGMATICS, II/2

The Bible has to be plundered and read for what it has to do with one's promise.

MARTIN E. MARTY
LUTHERAN PASTOR AND WRITER
YOU ARE A PROMISE, 1973

Has it ever struck you that the vast majority of the will of God for your life has already been revealed in the Bible? That is a crucial thing to grasp.

PAUL E. LITTLE (1928–1975)
AMERICAN EVANGELICAL LEADER

The Bible is the Book of books. The New Testament is a miracle of time. Read its spiritual heights and ethical pinnacles and remember the kind of men who wrote it. They were not generally learned or wise in man's wisdom, but they knew God and the way to God.

NELS F. S. FERRÉ
PROFESSOR OF PHILOSOPHICAL THEOLOGY
MAKING RELIGION REAL, 1956

How are the deep reaches of the self to be discerned and dealt with? . . .

Upon a realistic, critical, adult reading, by those prepared to be honest with their experience, the Bible incisively lays bare the depths and obscurities of the human heart. This is why it continues to play the decisive role it does in human history and culture and why it is fitted to be the perpetual instrument of the Spirit of God for human transformation . . .

DALLAS WILLARD
SOUTHERN BAPTIST MINISTER, THEOLOGIAN AND SCHOLAR
THE SPIRIT OF THE DISCIPLINES: UNDERSTANDING HOW GOD CHANGES LIVES, 1988

Unless we form the habit of going to the Bible in bright moments as well as in trouble, we cannot fully respond to its consolations because we lack equilibrium between light and darkness.

HELEN KELLER (1880-1968)
AMERICAN WRITER AND SOCIAL REFORMER
(BLIND AND DEAF FROM THE AGE OF 19 MONTHS)

The most remarkable thing, though, is the difference Scripture makes in the lives of those who sincerely follow it. I've never found anyone who said, "I've studied the Bible; I've lived it for years—and it doesn't work for me." The people I've talked to say that the more they truly absorb Scripture and seek to live by its precepts, they find that God is able to accomplish amazing things for his purposes through their lives.

CHARLES W. COLSON
FORMER WHITE HOUSE COUNSEL AND FOUNDER OF
PRISON FELLOWSHIP

I am a Bible-bigot. I follow it in all things, both great and small.

JOHN WESLEY (1703-1791)
ENGLISH PREACHER AND FOUNDER OF METHODISM
JOURNAL ENTRY, JUNE 1766

A knowledge of the Bible is essential to a rich and meaningful life. For the words of this Book have a way of filling in the missing pieces, of bridging the gaps, of turning the tarnished colors of our life into jewel-like brilliance.

BILLY GRAHAM (WILLIAM FRANKLIN GRAHAM JR.)
AMERICAN EVANGELICAL LEADER AND WRITER

Read a portion of the Scriptures, and offer prayer, if practicable, in every house or room you visit; if impracticable, introduce into your conversation as much of the Scriptures as possible, and see that the terms used are understood. In reading or speaking, let those portions that bear on the depravity of man, justification by faith alone, the necessity of a change of heart and of holiness of life, ever hold a prominent place.

LONDON CITY MISSION
INSTRUCTIONS TO MISSIONARIES, 1858

All our good consists in the way that we take advantage of His words.

ST. TERESA OF AVILA (1515-1582)
SPANISH MYSTIC CARMELITE NUN
THE INTERIOR CASTLE

All of us can try to live an average life—nothing special, but good enough to get along and to make us feel self-satisfied. But an important reason to study the Scriptures is to help each of us define and strive for a transcendent life—a life that reaches above and beyond what is normally expected of us. From Scripture, we can learn how Jesus Christ lived and what he set forth as proper priorities for human existence. We are aware of this opportunity in moments of exaltation or inspiration, when we are embarrassed by our own inadequacies, or perhaps when we are in total despair. The Bible offers concrete guidance for overcoming our weaknesses and striving toward the transcendent life for which we were created.

JIMMY CARTER (JAMES EARL CARTER)
PRESIDENT OF THE UNITED STATES
SOURCES OF STRENGTH: MEDITATIONS ON SCRIPTURE FOR A LIVING FAITH, 1997

When you read God's word, you must constantly be saying to yourself, "It is talking to me, and about me."

SOREN KIERKEGAARD (1813–1855)
DANISH PHILOSOPHER
FOR SELF-EXAMINATION, 1851

Do you know a book that you are willing to put
under your head for a pillow when you are dying?
Very well; that is the book you want to study when
you are living. There is only one such book
in the world.

JOSEPH COOK
QUOTED IN BILLY GRAHAM, *PEACE WITH GOD*, 1984

Other books were given for our information, the
Bible was given for our transformation.

T. H. DARLOW (THOMAS HERBERT DARLOW)
(1858-1927)
CONGREGATIONALIST THEOLOGIAN AND BIBLE SCHOLAR
THE DEFENDER

*D*o not merely listen to the word, and so deceive yourselves. Do
what it says.

JAMES 1:22

The POWER of the BIBLE to
ILLUMINATE CHRIST

The revelation of Jesus Christ, which God gave him to show his servants what must soon take place. He made it known by sending his angel to his servant John, who testifies to everything he saw— that is, the word of God and the testimony of Jesus Christ. Blessed is the one who reads the words of this prophecy, and blessed are those who hear it and take to heart what is written in it, because the time is near.

REVELATION 1:1–3

Our Christian conviction is that the Bible has both authority and relevance—to a degree quite extraordinary in so ancient a book—and that the secret of both is in Jesus Christ. Indeed, we should never think of the Christ and the Bible apart. . . .

This reciprocal testimony between the Living Word and the written Word is the clue to our Christian understanding of the Bible. For his testimony to it assures us of its authority, and its testimony to him of its relevance. The authority and the relevance are his.

JOHN R. W. STOTT
RECTOR EMERITUS OF ALL SOULS CHURCH, LONDON
THE AUTHORITY AND RELEVANCE OF THE BIBLE IN THE MODERN WORLD, 1979

Everything in the Christian Faith goes back ultimately to the story of Jesus recorded in the little books we call the Gospels. As all true Christian morality is based on the ethic of Jesus, so all sound Christian doctrine must be built on the person and work of Christ as they are presented to us in the Gospels.

A. M. HUNTER
PROFESSOR OF BIBLICAL CRITICISM
THE WORK AND WORDS OF JESUS, 1950

Jesus loves me—this I know
For the Bible tells me so.

SUSAN BOGERT WARNER (1819–1885)
AMERICAN NOVELIST AND HYMN WRITER
SONG, "THE LOVE OF JESUS"

These writings bring back to you the living image of
that most holy mind, the very Christ himself
speaking, healing, dying, rising, in fact so entirely
present, that you would see less of him if you beheld
him with your eyes.

ELIZABETH I (1533-1603)
QUEEN OF ENGLAND FROM 1558

Thanks be to the gospel, by means of which we also,
who did not see Christ when he came into this
world, seem to be with Him when we
read his deeds.

ST. AMBROSE (C.339-397)
BISHOP OF MILAN AND CHURCH FATHER

Scripture is full of Christ. From Genesis to
Revelation everything breathes of Him, not every
letter of every sentence, but the spirit of
every chapter.

FREDERICK W. ROBERTSON (1816-1853)
ENGLISH PREACHER

His teaching surpasseth all teaching of holy men, and
such as have His Spirit find therein the hidden
manna. But there are many who, though they

frequently hear the Gospel, yet feel but little longing after it, because they have not the mind of Christ. He, therefore, that will fully and with true wisdom understand the words of Christ, let him strive to conform his whole life to that mind of Christ.

THOMAS À KEMPIS (C.1380–1471)
GERMAN MONK, MYSTIC AND WRITER
THE IMITATION OF CHRIST

All that I am I owe to Jesus Christ, revealed to me in His divine Book.

DAVID LIVINGSTONE (1813–1873)
SCOTTISH DOCTOR, MISSIONARY AND EXPLORER OF AFRICA

Christ is the key to the Scriptures. . . . Christ is the center of the economy of salvation, the recapitulation of the Old and New Testaments, of the promises of the Law and of their fulfillment in the Gospel; he is the living and eternal link between the Old and New Covenants.

POPE JOHN PAUL II (1920–2005)
POLISH PRIEST AND PHILOSOPHER
ENCYCLICAL LETTER *VERITATIS SPLENDOR*, 1993

God the Father is the giver of Holy Scripture; God the Son is the theme of holy Scripture; and God the Spirit is the author, authenticator, and interpreter of Holy Scripture.

JAMES I. PACKER
BRITISH EVANGELICAL THEOLOGIAN AND WRITER

When our minds find inner agreement with the truth expressed in the passages, we embrace the mind of Christ as *our own*, for these great Scriptural truths are the very things Jesus believed. These truths constitute the faith, hope and love in which He lived. And as they become ours, His mind becomes our mind. Then we become true co-laborers with God, as brothers, sisters and friends of Jesus in the present and coming Kingdom of God. We can then know and understand in its fullness the *guidance* God gives to His children.

DALLAS WILLARD
SOUTHERN BAPTIST MINISTER, THEOLOGIAN AND SCHOLAR
PRAYING THE SCRIPTURES, 1998

Christ sent me to preach the gospel and he will look after the results.

MARY SLESSOR (1848–1915)
SCOTTISH MISSIONARY TO WEST AFRICA

We must hear Jesus speak if we expect him
to hear us speak.

CHARLES HADDON SPURGEON (1834–1892)
ENGLISH NONCONFORMIST PREACHER
(REPUTED TO BE ONE OF THE GREATEST PREACHERS
OF ALL TIME)

Whatever view of the Bible you take, if you are to
be in any way obedient to the Bible you cannot
make the Bible itself the centre or focus of your
attention. It points away from itself. From the
Christian point of view, the centre of attention can
never be merely the Bible; it must always be
Jesus of Nazareth, Jesus the Messiah,
Jesus the Lord of the World.

TOM WRIGHT
BISHOP OF DURHAM AND VICE-PRESIDENT OF
THE BIBLE SOCIETY

Our Lord Jesus Christ, the word of God, of his
boundless love, became what we are that he might
make us what he himself is.

IRANAEUS (130–202)
BISHOP OF LYONS

It takes time to grow into Jesus the Vine; do not expect to abide in Him unless you will give Him that time. It is not enough to read God's Word, or meditations as here offered. . . . Therefore, my brother who wants to learn to abide in Jesus, take time each day, before you read, while you read, and after you read, to put yourself into living contact with the living Jesus, to yield yourself distinctly and consciously to His blessed influence, so will you give Him the opportunity of taking hold of you, of drawing you up and keeping you safe in His almighty life.

ANDREW MURRAY (1828–1917)
PASTOR AND AUTHOR IN SOUTH AFRICA AND SCOTLAND
ABIDE IN CHRIST, 1895

Standing on the promises of Christ my King,
Thro' eternal ages let His praises ring;
Glory in the highest, I will shout and sing,
Standing on the promises of God.
Standing, standing,
Standing on the promises of God my Savior;
Standing, standing,
I'm standing on the promises of God.

R. KELSO CARTER (1849–1926)
METHODIST MINISTER
HYMN, "STANDING ON THE PROMISES"

. . . God's Word, which is all about Jesus Christ, can do for us what we cannot do for ourselves. We are sinful and unable to remedy our condition, but from God comes the incredible, limitless power that can transform our lives.

JOHN MACARTHUR
TRUTH FOR TODAY, 2001

It seems to me that our greatest need today is an enlarged vision of Jesus Christ. We need to see him as the One in whom alone the fullness of God dwells and in whom alone we can come to fullness of life . . .

There is only one way to gain clear, true, fresh, lofty views of Christ, and that is through the Bible. The Bible is the prism by which the light of Jesus Christ is broken into its many and beautiful colors. The Bible is the portrait of Jesus Christ. We need to gaze upon him with such intensity of desire that (by the gracious work of the Holy Spirit) he comes alive to us, meets with us, and fills us with himself.

JOHN R. W. STOTT
RECTOR EMERITUS OF ALL SOULS CHURCH, LONDON
UNDERSTANDING THE BIBLE, 1999

Our one desire for all the Church's children is that, being saturated with the Bible, they may arrive at the all-surpassing knowledge of Jesus Christ.

POPE BENEDICT XV (1854–1922)
ENCYCLICAL LETTER *ON ST. JEROME*, 1920

On the third day he rose again
in accordance with the Scriptures;
he ascended into heaven
and is seated at the right hand of the Father.
He will come again in glory to judge the living and the dead,
and his kingdom will have no end.

THE NICENE CREED
PROFESSION OF THE CHRISTIAN FAITH ADOPTED AT THE
COUNCIL OF CONSTANTINOPLE, 381

After reading the doctrines of Plato, Socrates, or Aristotle, we feel that the specific difference between their words and Christ's is the difference between an inquiry and a revelation.

JOSEPH PARKER (1830–1902)
ENGLISH CONGREGATIONALIST PREACHER AND
BIBLE COMMENTATOR

Have your eyes ever been opened to see the glorious excellency of Jesus Christ? Has the light of the Word of God ever shined into your hearts so that to see the excellency of the Word that teaches Christ and the way of Salvation by him? Has the Word of Christ been sweeter to you than the honey on the honeycomb?

JONATHAN EDWARDS (1703–1758)
AMERICAN THEOLOGIAN
"WHAT IS MEANT BY BELIEVING IN CHRIST," 1752 SERMON TO
THE MOHAWK INDIANS

Read the prophetic books without seeing Christ in them, and how flat and insipid they are! See Christ there, and what you read is fragrant.

JOHN CHRYSOSTOM (c.347–407)
ARCHBISHOP OF CONSTANTINOPLE AND CHURCH FATHER

We may compare the Bible to the Old Testament Tabernacle in the wilderness with its three courts. The outer court is the letter of the Scriptures; the inner court, or holy place, is the truth of the Scriptures; the holiest place of all is the person of Jesus Christ; and only when we pass the inmost veil do we come to him.

ARTHUR T. PIERSON (1837–1911)
AMERICAN PRESBYTERIAN MINISTER

If an earthly king—our tsar—wrote you a letter, would
you not read it with joy? Certainly, with great
rejoicing and careful attention. The King of heaven
has sent a letter to you, an earthly and mortal man;
yet you almost despise such a gift, so priceless a
treasure. Whenever you read the Gospel, Christ
himself is speaking with you. And while you read,
you are praying and talking with him.

TIKHON OF ZADONSK (1724–1783)
RUSSIAN ORTHODOX BISHOP

The Bible has been so many words to us—clouds and
darkness—then all of a sudden the words become
spirit and full of life because Jesus re-speaks them to
us in a particular condition. That is the way God
speaks to us, not by visions and dreams, but by
words. When a man gets to God it is by the most
simple way of words.

OSWALD CHAMBERS (1874–1917)
SCOTTISH EVANGELIST AND WRITER
MY UTMOST FOR HIS HIGHEST

The value of the gospel is not that it gives us ideal
life, but that that life was actually lived.

GEORGE TYRELL (1861–1909)
IRISH THEOLOGIAN

I am pleased for my brothers to study the Scriptures so long as they do not neglect application to prayer, after the example of Christ, of whom we read that he prayed more than he read.

ST. FRANCIS OF ASSISI (1182–1226)
ITALIAN FOUNDER OF THE FRANCISCAN ORDER

All Sacred Scripture is but one book, and that one book is Christ, because all divine Scripture speaks of Christ, and all divine Scripture is fulfilled in Christ.

HUGH OF ST. VICTOR (1096–1141)
GERMAN-BORN MONK AND WRITER

A social style characterized by the creation of a new community and the rejection of violence of any kind is the theme of New Testament proclamation from beginning to end, from right to left. The cross of Christ is the model of Christian social efficacy, the power of God for those who believe.

JOHN HOWARD YODER (1927–1997)
AMERICAN MENNONITE THEOLOGIAN AND PROFESSOR
THE POLITICS OF JESUS, 1972

The four gospels are essential to our understanding
of who Jesus was and what he taught and did, and
therefore they are fundamental to our understanding
of Christianity. . . . Put out of your mind the Sunday
School image of a smiling Jesus carrying a lamb on
his shoulders through a summer meadow. Imagine
instead a kindly but forthright person surrounded by
an angry mob in a narrow Near Eastern back street,
telling them that they've had their religion wrong for
centuries and that he alone has got it right. . . .

DEREK WILLIAMS
THE BIBLE APPLICATION HANDBOOK, 1999

The only proper response to this word which Jesus
brings with him from eternity is simply to do it.
Jesus has spoken: his is the word, ours is the
obedience. Only in the doing of it does the word of
Jesus attain its honor, might, and power among us.

DIETRICH BONHOEFFER (1905-1945)
GERMAN THEOLOGIAN
THE COST OF DISCIPLESHIP, 1937

The Word of God was not made for us; rather we
were made for him.

ATHANASIUS (C.296-373)
BISHOP OF ALEXANDRIA AND CHURCH FATHER

As we spend time reading, applying, and obeying our Bibles, the Spirit of Truth Who is also the Spirit of Jesus increasingly reveals Jesus to us.

ANNE GRAHAM LOTZ
BIBLE TEACHER AND FOUNDER OF ANGEL MINISTRIES

Christ has been too long locked up in the mass or in the Book; let him be your prophet, priest and king. Obey him.

GEORGE FOX (1624-1691)
ENGLISH FOUNDER OF THE SOCIETY OF FRIENDS
(THE QUAKERS)

As I continued along the Way, I learned, step by step, word by word, that behind every saying in the Gospels stands one man and one man's experience. Also the prayer that the cup might pass from him and his promise to drink it. Also behind each of the words from the Cross.

DAG HAMMARSKJOLD (1905-1961)
SWEDISH STATESMAN AND SECRETARY GENERAL OF
THE UNITED NATIONS
MARKINGS, 1963

Christ is the focus of the entire Bible, and you need to study it to know what He is like. Too often we study the Bible for the sake of theological arguments or to answer questions. Those things are important, but the main point of Bible study is to know more about Christ so that you can be like him.

JOHN MACARTHUR
TRUTH FOR TODAY, 2001

The foundations of Christian ethics must be evangelical foundations; or, to put it more simply, Christian ethics must arise from the gospel of Jesus Christ. Otherwise it could not be *Christian* ethics.

OLIVER M. T. O'DONOVAN
REGIUS PROFESSOR OF MORAL AND PASTORAL THEOLOGY AT
OXFORD UNIVERSITY
RESURRECTION AND THE MORAL ORDER, 1994

I believe in Christ's teaching; this is what I believe. I believe that my welfare in the world will only be possible when all men fulfill Christ's teaching.

LEO TOLSTOY (1828–1910)
RUSSIAN NOVELIST
WHAT I BELIEVE, 1884

The Bible is a great love story. It describes how, despite our disobedience and indifference, God persevered with the human race. Indeed, "God loved the world so much that he gave his only Son." (John 3:16) The Bible is also a book about a battle: it describes a cosmic struggle between good and evil. That great struggle finds its focus in Jesus Christ. We read that darkness and light, love and hatred, compassion and indifference have contended and that he—Jesus—is Victor, Lord and King.

JOHN YOUNG
CANON OF YORK MINSTER
TEACH YOURSELF CHRISTIANITY, 1999

All glory be to thee, Almighty God, our heavenly Father, for that thou, of thy tender mercy, didst give thine only Son Jesus Christ to suffer death upon the cross for our redemption, who made there, by his one oblation of himself once offered, a full, perfect, and sufficient sacrifice, oblation, and satisfaction, for the sins of the whole world; and did institute, and in his holy Gospel command us to continue, a perpetual memory of that his precious death and sacrifice, until his coming again.

FIRST EUCHARISTIC PRAYER
THE EPISCOPAL CHURCH OF AMERICA

Every word of the Bible rings with Christ.

MARTIN LUTHER (1485-1546)
GERMAN MONK, THEOLOGIAN AND LEADER OF THE
PROTESTANT REFORMATION

If you find something that speaks to your condition,
becomes authoritative, then roll it over and over in
the mind. Rolling it over in the mind, it will become
an atmosphere, then an attitude, then an act. When
Jesus was pressed by temptation in the wilderness
He answered in the words of Scripture. These words
had become a part of Him, and in the crisis they
naturally passed from the stage of assimilation and
atmosphere to that of attitude and act.

E. STANLEY JONES (1884-1972)
MISSIONARY AND EVANGELIST
ABUNDANT LIVING, 1946

. . . The Bible is the most important document that
we have, because it is at one and the same time a
progressive revelation of the love of God and the
epitome of that revelation in the spirit and teaching
of Jesus Christ, who is not only the man who died
on the cross, but the living interpretation, the human
photograph, of God.

LORD SOPER (DONALD) (1903-1998)
BRITISH METHODIST MINISTER

Mel Gibson's latest film *The Passion of the Christ* is a harrowing insight into the last twelve hours of the life of Jesus of Nazareth. It portrays in graphic and moving detail the arrest, trial, torture and execution of this controversial figure whose life and teaching have inspired the devotion of billions in the two thousand years since he lived and died in Palestine. . . . The Bible writers see that the Passion of Jesus reveals something of far deeper significance than a stirring example—a meaning that has equally deep significance for each one of us today.

"THE PASSION OF JESUS CHRIST: ITS MEANING FOR TODAY," 2004
BOOKLET FROM THE GOOD BOOK COMPANY

The Bible sanctifies and molds the mind into the image of Christ.

CHARLES HADDON SPURGEON (1834–1892)
ENGLISH NONCONFORMIST PREACHER
(REPUTED TO BE ONE OF THE GREATEST PREACHERS
OF ALL TIME)

In the Old Testament, we have Jesus predicted. In the Gospels, we have Jesus revealed. In the Acts, we have Jesus preached. In the Epistles, we have Jesus explained. In the revelation, we have Jesus expected.

ALISTAIR BEGG
SCOTTISH PASTOR, EVANGELIST AND BROADCASTER

The Father, dwelling in the depths of all things and in my own depths, communicates to me His Word and His Spirit. Receiving them I am drawn into His own life and know God in His own Love, being one with Him in His own Son.

THOMAS MERTON (1915–1968)
FRENCH-BORN TRAPPIST MONK AND POET
SEEDS OF CONTEMPLATION, 1961

In different times and places, Christians have responded in diverse ways to Jesus, and the distinct pictures of him in the gospels have found their favour accordingly. Those who feel his impact have found themselves attracted, fascinated, challenged, uplifted, and changed. To them, Jesus is human yet uniquely open to and inspired by God, so that in him the eternal God comes near.

CAMBRIDGE ILLUSTRATED HISTORY OF RELIGIONS, 2002

Ignorance of the Scripture is ignorance of Christ.

ST. JEROME (C.342–420)
DALMATIAN-BORN CHURCH FATHER
(TRANSLATOR OF ORIGINAL-LANGUAGE TEXTS INTO THE
LATIN BIBLE VERSION KNOWN AS *THE VULGATE*)

The fact of Jesus Christ is the eternal message of the Bible. It is the story of life, peace, eternity, and heaven. The Bible has no hidden purpose. It has no need for special interpretation. It has a single, clear, bold message for every living being—the message of Christ and His offer of peace with God.

BILLY GRAHAM (WILLIAM FRANKLIN GRAHAM JR.)
AMERICAN EVANGELICAL LEADER AND WRITER
PEACE WITH GOD, 1953

The Scriptures and the words of Jesus possess a terrible power in themselves and a wonderful sweetness. Straightaway a flame was kindled in my soul, and a love of the prophets and of those men who were friends of Christ possessed me.

JUSTIN MARTYR (c.100–165)
CHRISTIAN APOLOGIST

These are the Scriptures that testify about me . . .

JOHN 5:39

The POWER of the BIBLE to
REVEAL TRUTH

*J*esus said, "If you hold to my teaching, you are really my disciples. Then you will know the truth, and the truth will set you free."

JOHN 8:31-32

It is one thing to be told that the Bible has authority because it is divinely inspired, and another thing to feel one's heart leap out and grasp its truth.

LESLIE D. WEATHERHEAD (1893–1976)
BRITISH METHODIST MINISTER
THE CHRISTIAN AGNOSTIC, 1965

All human discoveries seem to be made only for the purpose of confirming more and more strongly the truths contained in the Sacred Scriptures.

SIR WILLIAM HERSCHEL (1738–1822)
GERMAN-BORN ENGLISH ASTRONOMER

Because God does not speak to us every day from the heavens, and there are only the Scriptures alone, in which he has willed that his truth shall be published and made known unto even the end, they can be fully certified to the faithful by no other warrant than this: that we hold it to be decreed and concluded that they came down from heaven, as though we heard God speaking from his own mouth.

JOHN CALVIN (1509–1564)
FRENCH-BORN REFORMED THEOLOGIAN

The only way we can discern the true from the false is to know the Shepherd's voice—God's Word. One of the primary reasons we need to be in a disciplined study of the Scriptures is so we can saturate ourselves in the truth. When we know the truth and we are presented with that which is false, we will instinctively recognize it. Measuring philosophies or theologies or opinions or sermons or books or doctrines or counsel by the Word of God is like exposing the crookedness of a stick by placing a straight stick beside it.

ANNE GRAHAM LOTZ
BIBLE TEACHER AND FOUNDER OF ANGEL MINISTRIES
MY HEART'S CRY: LONGING FOR MORE OF JESUS, 2002

Truth: That which is real and reliable; opposite of falsehood and error; descriptive of the divine Father, Son and Holy Spirit as the full revelation of the one true God.

GLOSSARY OF THEOLOGICAL TERMS
NIV DISCIPLE'S STUDY BIBLE, 1988

Men turn this way and that in their search for new sources of comfort and inspiration, but the enduring truths are to be found in the Word of God.

ELIZABETH, THE QUEEN MOTHER (1900-2002)
BRITISH QUEEN CONSORT

Therefore, since everything asserted by the inspired authors or sacred writers must be held to be asserted by the Holy Spirit, it follows that the books of scripture must be acknowledged as teaching firmly, faithfully, and without error that truth which God wanted put in the sacred writings for the sake of our salvation.

SECOND VATICAN COUNCIL
DOGMATIC CONSTITUTION ON DIVINE REVELATION, 1965

. . . You may read some of the teachings of Jesus, in, for example, the Sermon on the Mount, hundreds of times and they are just sayings with little apparent meaning for you. And then one day, suddenly, one of them comes to life for you. It strikes you as a statement of inexorable, absolute, undeniable truth.

A. GORDON JONES
WHAT DID JESUS TEACH? 1969

Much of listening, then, means heeding what God has already revealed. We have something against which the aberrations of our own spiritual eccentricities can be measured, corrected. We read and hear the Bible's words and stories not just for information, but for truth about God, Jesus and the Holy Spirit.

TIMOTHY JONES
AWAKE MY SOUL: PRACTICAL SPIRITUALITY FOR BUSY PEOPLE,
2000

. . . The perfect infallibility of the Scriptures in every part, as a record of fact and doctrine both in thought and in verbal expression. So though they come to us through the instrumentality of minds, hearts, imaginations, consciences and wills of men, they are nevertheless in the strictest sense the word of God.

A. A. HODGE (1823-1886)
AMERICAN PRESBYTERIAN CLERGYMAN AND EDUCATOR

We search the world for truth; we cull
The good, the pure, the beautiful,
From graven stone and written scroll
From all the old flower-fields of the soul;
And, weary seekers of the best,
We come back laden from our quest,
To find that all the sages said
Is in the Book our mothers read.

JOHN GREENLEAF WHITTIER (1807–1892)
AMERICAN POET
"MIRIAM"

What God's Son has told me, take for true I do;
Truth himself speaks truly or there's nothing true.

ST. THOMAS AQUINAS (1225–1274)
ITALIAN DOMINICAN FRIAR, THEOLOGIAN AND DOCTOR OF
THE CHURCH

We cannot attain to the understanding of Scripture
either by study or by the intellect. Your first duty is
to begin by prayer. Entreat the Lord to grant you, of
His great mercy, the true understanding of His
Word.

MARTIN LUTHER (1485–1546)
GERMAN MONK, THEOLOGIAN AND LEADER OF THE
PROTESTANT REFORMATION

I have been suspected of being what is called a Fundamentalist. That is because I never regard any narrative as unhistorical simply on the ground that it includes the miraculous.

C. S. LEWIS (CLIVE STAPLES LEWIS) (1898-1963)
IRISH LITERARY SCHOLAR, CHRISTIAN APOLOGIST
AND WRITER
THE JOYFUL CHRISTIAN, 1977

The Bible, as a creative work of men analogous to the Creation of God and inspired by the same Creator, is possible on the basis of the *imago Dei*—of the truth revealed in Genesis 1 and 2 that man is made in God's image. Only on the basis of this truth could God's Spirit be able to move through certain chosen human authors and in a sense make manifest in human words God's Very Word and His ways with men.

GEORGE HOBSON
CANON THEOLOGIAN, AMERICAN CATHEDRAL IN PARIS

. . . It is impossible that God Himself, the supreme Truth, can utter that which is not true. This is the ancient and unchanging faith of the church. . . .

POPE LEO XIII (1810-1903)
ENCYCLICAL LETTER *ON THE STUDY OF HOLY SCRIPTURE*, 1893

Like Joseph storing up grain during the years of
plenty to be used during the years of famine that lay
ahead, may we store up the truth of God's Word in
our hearts as much as possible, so that we are
prepared for whatever suffering we are called
upon to endure.

BILLY GRAHAM (WILLIAM FRANKLIN GRAHAM JR.)
AMERICAN EVANGELICAL LEADER AND WRITER
TILL ARMAGEDDON, 1981

Beyond the sacred page I seek Thee, Lord;
My spirit pants for Thee, O Living Word.
O send Thy Spirit, Lord, now unto me,
That he may touch my eyes, and make me see;
Show me the truth concealed in Thy Word,
And in Thy book revealed, I see Thee Lord.

MARY ARTEMISIA LATHBURY (1841-1913)
HYMN, "BREAK THOU THE BREAD OF LIFE"

The biblical view of knowledge is both at odds with
and the solution to the more widely accepted
humanistic view expressed throughout Western
history. By revealing Himself God clears our vision,
heals the damage done by sin to His image within,
and makes us capable of true knowledge and

wisdom. . . . Our task is not to *establish* truth but rather to *recognize* God's truth and live obediently under it.

W. ANDREW HOFFECKER AND G. K. BEALE
BUILDING A CHRISTIAN WORLD VIEW, 1986

The Word of God is true because God himself will make it true in us. You have much to learn, much to overcome, and much to surrender to see that power. But this will come about if you will approach your Bible study determined that God's Word has omnipotent power to work out every blessing it promises.

ANDREW MURRAY (1828–1917)
PREACHER AND AUTHOR IN SOUTH AFRICA AND SCOTLAND

Believe God's word and power more than you believe your own feelings and experiences.

SAMUEL RUTHERFORD (C.1600–1661)
SCOTTISH PRESBYTERIAN MINISTER

Comfort in tribulation can be secured only on the sure ground of faith holding as true the words of Scripture and the teaching of the Church.

THOMAS MORE (1478–1535)
ENGLISH STATESMAN AND MARTYR

O Word of God Incarnate,
O Wisdom from on high,
O Truth unchanged, unchanging,
O Light of our dark sky;
We praise Thee for the radiance
That from the hallowed page,
A lantern to our footsteps,
Shines on from age to age.

WILLIAM W. HOW (1823–1897)
ENGLISH BISHOP AND HYMN WRITER
HYMN, "O WORD OF GOD INCARNATE"

The best evidence of the Bible's being the word of
God is to be found between its covers.
It proves itself.

CHARLES HODGE (1797–1878)
PROFESSOR AT PRINCETON THEOLOGICAL SEMINARY

The Holy Scripture is the only sufficient, certain,
and infallible rule of all saving knowledge, faith,
and obedience. . . .

SECOND WESTMINSTER CONFESSION, 1677

Explain the Scriptures by the Scriptures.

CLEMENT OF ALEXANDRIA (C.150–215)
CHURCH FATHER

The Christian believes that Scripture has something to say to the world and to mankind and that something carries authority. However, biblical authority does not rest with the pages of the Bible itself. This is no paper-Pope. Biblical authority stems from its relationship with God.

DAVID COOK
DIRECTOR OF THE WHITEFIELD INSTITUTE IN OXFORD
THE MORAL MAZE–A WAY OF EXPLORING CHRISTIAN ETHICS,
1983

It is a certain truth, that none can understand the prophets' and apostles' writings aright, without the same Spirit by which they were written.

GEORGE FOX (1624–1691)
ENGLISH FOUNDER OF THE SOCIETY OF FRIENDS
(THE QUAKERS)

I believe that the intention of Holy Writ was to persuade men of the truths necessary to salvation; such as neither science nor other means could render credible, but only the voice of the Holy Spirit.

GALILEO GALILEI (1564–1642)
ITALIAN SCIENTIST
LETTER TO FATHER BERNEDETTO CASTELLI, 1613

The truth of the Gospel, which is essentially and initially a corporate possession, is personally appropriated by prayer in the heart of the believer.

JOHN BYROM (1692-1763)
ENGLISH HYMN WRITER

So often we have a kind of vague, wistful longing that the promises of Jesus should be true. The only way really to enter into them is to believe them with the clutching intensity of a drowning man.

WILLIAM BARCLAY
SCOTTISH THEOLOGIAN, RELIGIOUS WRITER
AND BROADCASTER

Whence but from Heaven, could men unskill'd
in arts
In several ages born, in several parts,
Weave such agreeing truths? Or how or why
Should all conspire to cheat us with a lie?
Unasked their pains, ungrateful their advice,
Starving their gain, and martyrdom their price.

JOHN DRYDEN (1631-1701)
ENGLISH POET AND DRAMATIST
"RELIGIO LAICI"

Approaching one young man, I held up my Bible and asked, "Do you believe the Bible is the Word of God?"

"Yes!" he said with confidence and conviction.

I probed him further. "Do you believe the Bible is true?"

"Yes!" rang the answer again.

Then I asked, "Is it historically accurate and reliable?"

"Of course!" he replied with confidence.

Then I lowered my voice and asked him, "Why?"

He looked back at me, shrugged his shoulders, and said, "That's a tough one."

JOSH McDOWELL AND THOMAS WILLIAMS
IN SEARCH OF CERTAINTY, 2003

The word of God is plain in itself; and if there appear any obscurity in one place, the Holy Ghost, which is never contrarious to himself, explains the same more clearly in other places.

JOHN KNOX (1505–1572)
SCOTTISH PROTESTANT REFORMER

What is the mark of a Christian? Faith working by love. What is the mark of faith? Unhesitating conviction of the truth of the inspired words, unshaken by any argument either based on the plea of physical necessity or masquerading in the guise of piety. What is the mark of a believer? To hold fast by such conviction in the strength of what Scripture says and to dare neither to set it at nought nor to add to it.

BASIL OF CAESAREA (330-379)
BISHOP AND CHURCH FATHER

And although there are various ideas taught in the main books of the gospel, it makes no difference to the faith of believers, since all things are set out in each of them, by the one Spirit, concerning the birth, passion, resurrection, the conversation with the disciples, and [Christ's] two comings, one in humility and the other to be in the future, in royal power.

MURATORIAN FRAGMENT (c.190)
(OLDEST KNOWN LISTING OF THE BOOKS OF THE NEW
TESTAMENT, DISCOVERED BY L. A. MURATORI IN 1740)

The right way of interpreting scripture is to take it as we find it, without any attempts to force it into any particular system.

RICHARD CECIL (1748–1810)
ANGLICAN PREACHER

Inspiration is the name of that all-comprehensive operation of the Holy Spirit whereby he has bestowed on the church a complete and infallible Scripture.

ABRAHAM KUYPER (1837–1920)
DUTCH CALVINIST THEOLOGIAN AND POLITICIAN

When the consensus of scholarship says one thing and the Word of God another, the consensus of scholarship can plumb go to hell for all I care.

BILLY SUNDAY (WILLIAM A. SUNDAY) (1862–1935)
AMERICAN EVANGELIST

The authority of Scripture must be followed in all things, for in it we have the truth as it were in its secret haunts.

JOHN SCOTUS ERIGENA (C.810–877)
IRISH PHILOSOPHER

There is no substitute for the reading of the Bible. . . . Theologically it is the standard for Christian thought. I believe, in fact, that it is the standard for all thought, for its central truths are eternal: the living God, who creates and rules the world, the law of love as seen in matchless depth and vividness in the life, teachings and death of Jesus, and the law of life witnessed to by his healings and his resurrection.

NELS F. S. FERRÉ
PROFESSOR OF PHILOSOPHICAL THEOLOGY
MAKING RELIGION REAL, 1956

I wish to show that there is one wisdom which is perfect, and that this is contained in the Scriptures.

SIR FRANCIS BACON (1561-1626)
ENGLISH LAWYER, PHILOSOPHER AND ESSAYIST

First, we can know the Bible is reliable because Jesus said it was reliable.

NORMAN GEISLER
CHRISTIAN APOLOGIST AND WRITER

Be astounded that God should have written to us.

ST. ANTONY OF EGYPT (C.251-356)
EGYPTIAN ASCETIC

This truth and discipline are contained in the written books, and in the unwritten traditions which, received by the apostles from the mouth of Christ himself, or from the apostles themselves, the Holy Spirit dictating, have come down to us, transmitted as it were from hand to hand. . . . and preserved in the Catholic Church by a continuous succession.

THE COUNCIL OF TRENT, 1546
(CATHOLIC AFFIRMATION THAT BOTH SCRIPTURE AND
TRADITION ARE SOURCES OF REVELATION)

We believe that the Word contained in these books has proceeded from God, and receives its authority from him alone, and not from human beings. And in that it is the rule of all truth, containing all that is necessary for the service of God and for our salvation, it is not lawful for anyone, even for angels, to add to it, to take away from it, or to change it.

FRENCH CONFESSION OF FAITH (*CONFESSIO GALLICANA*), 1559
(PROTESTANT AFFIRMATION THAT THE AUTHORITY OF
SCRIPTURE IS INHERENT IN THE BIBLE)

No sciences are better attested than the religion of the Bible.

SIR ISAAC NEWTON (1642–1727)
ENGLISH MATHEMATICIAN AND PHYSICIST

The first and most important book we are to study is the Bible. . . . When we study a book of the Bible we are seeking to be controlled by the intent of the author. We are determined to hear what he is saying, not what we want him to say. We want life-transforming truth, not just good feelings. We are willing to pay the price of barren day after barren day until the meaning is clear. This process revolutionizes our lives.

RICHARD J. FOSTER
QUAKER THEOLOGIAN AND WRITER
CELEBRATION OF DISCIPLINE, 1978

When we "believe in the Bible," we mean that it is more than just intellectually true. We proclaim that its truth has life-changing implications.

R. C. SPROUL
PROFESSOR OF THEOLOGY AND CHAIRMAN OF
LIGONIER MINISTRIES
FIVE THINGS EVERY CHRISTIAN NEEDS TO GROW, 2002

The Holy Scriptures given by inspiration of God are of themselves sufficient to the discovery of the truth.

ATHANASIUS (C.296–373)
BISHOP OF ALEXANDRIA AND CHURCH FATHER

. . . Scripture in its unity and totality is the objectification of God's irreversible and victorious offer of salvation to the world in Jesus Christ, and therefore in its unity and totality it cannot lead one away from God's truth in some binding way.

KARL RAHNER (1904-1984)
GERMAN ROMAN CATHOLIC THEOLOGIAN
FOUNDATIONS OF THE CHRISTIAN FAITH, 1978

God is not silent. It is in the nature of God to speak. The second person of the Trinity is called "The Word." The Bible is the inevitable outcome of God's continuous speech. It is the infallible declaration of His mind.

A. W. TOZER (AIDEN WILSON TOZER) (1897-1963)
AMERICAN PASTOR AND WRITER

Lord, thy word abideth
And our footsteps guideth;
Who its truth believeth
Light and joy receiveth.

HENRY WILLIAMS BAKER (1821-1877)
ENGLISH CLERGYMAN AND HYMN WRITER
HYMN, "LORD, THY WORD ABIDETH," 1861

There can be no falsehood anywhere in the literal
sense of Holy Scripture.

ST. THOMAS AQUINAS (1225–1274)
ITALIAN DOMINICAN FRIAR, THEOLOGIAN AND DOCTOR OF
THE CHURCH

I esteem the Gospels to be thoroughly genuine, for
there shines forth from them the reflected splendor
of a sublimity proceeding from the person of Jesus
Christ, and of as Divine a king as was ever
manifested upon the earth.

JOHANN WOLFGANG VON GOETHE (1749–1832)
GERMAN POET AND NOVELIST

The Spirit breathes upon the word,
And brings the truth to sight;
Precepts and promises afford
A sanctifying light.

WILLIAM COWPER (1731–1800)
ENGLISH POET, HYMN WRITER AND TRANSLATOR
"THE LIGHT AND GLORY OF THE LORD"

The Gospel is within you, and you are its evidence; it
is preached to you in your own bosom, and
everything within you is a proof of the truth of it.

WILLIAM LAW (1686–1761)
ENGLISH CONTEMPLATIVE AND CLERIC

I long to understand to some degree your truth,
which my heart believes and loves. For I do not seek
to understand in order that I may believe, but I
believe in order that I may understand.

ST. ANSELM (1033–1109)
ITALIAN-BORN MONK, SCHOLAR AND ARCHBISHOP
OF CANTERBURY

I have chosen the way of truth; I have set my heart on your laws.

PSALM 119:30

The POWER of the BIBLE to
INSPIRE THE
IMAGINATION

*I*n the beginning was the Word, and the Word was with God, and the Word was God. He was with God in the beginning.

Through him all things were made; without him nothing was made that has been made. In him was life, and that life was the light of men. The light shines in the darkness, but the darkness has not understood it.

JOHN 1:1-5

Holy Scripture excels all branches of learning in the very way it speaks; for with one and the same expression, it recounts history and utters a mystery.

ST. GREGORY THE GREAT (540-604)
POPE, CHURCH FATHER AND TEACHER

Some books are copper, some are silver, and some few are gold: but the Bible alone is like a book all made up of bank notes.

JOHN NEWTON (1725-1807)
EVANGELICAL HYMN WRITER AND FORMER SLAVE TRADER

Nobody ever outgrows Scripture; the book widens and deepens with our years.

CHARLES HADDON SPURGEON (1834-1892)
ENGLISH NONCONFORMIST PREACHER
(REPUTED TO BE ONE OF THE GREATEST PREACHERS
OF ALL TIME)

The two great qualities of the Authorized Version are simplicity and majesty. . . . As well as being for more than three centuries the most widely accepted rendering of the scriptures throughout the English-speaking world, the Authorized Version was to become a classic of the English language. Countless original phrases from the 1611 Bible passed into standard idiomatic English and remain a vivid part of our speech and writing today.

CAMBRIDGE BIBLE HANDBOOK, 1997

Our language has received innumerable elegancies
and improvements . . . out of the poetical passages in
Holy Writ. They give a force and energy to our
expression, warm and animate our language, and
convey our thoughts in more ardent and intense
phrases, than any that are to be met with in
our own tongue.

JOSEPH ADDISON (1672–1719)
ENGLISH ESSAYIST AND POET
THE SPECTATOR, 1712

No creature has meaning without the Word of God.
God's Word is in all creation, visible and invisible.
The Word is living, being, spirit, all verdant
greening, all creativity.
The Word flashes out in every creature.
This is how the spirit is in the flesh—the Word is
indivisible from God.

HILDEGARD OF BINGEN (1098–1179)
GERMAN NUN, POET AND VISIONARY
"GOD'S WORD IS IN ALL CREATION"

If God drew up his Bible to heaven and sent me
down another, it would not be newer to me.

WILLIAM GRIMSHAW (1708–1763)
ENGLISH CLERGYMAN

I think the Psalms are like a mirror, in which one
can see oneself and the movements of
one's own heart.

ATHANASIUS (296–373)
BISHOP OF ALEXANDRIA

What a book! Great and wide as the world, rooted in
the abysmal depths of creation and rising aloft into
the blue mysteries of heaven. Sunrise and sunset,
promise and fulfillment, birth and death, the whole
human drama: everything is in this book. It is the
book of books, *Biblia*.

HEINRICH HEINE (1797–1856)
GERMAN POET

Christians need no other reason to be avid readers of
the Word of God. Realizing that Scripture is "God-
breathed" is motivation enough. . . . When the mind
and spirit of a biblical author interact in vibrant
dialogue with the mind and spirit of the reader, the
highest purpose of the inspired Word is fulfilled.
We should soar every time we read
the Word of God.

DAVID L. McKENNA
UNIVERSITY PRESIDENT
HOW TO READ A CHRISTIAN BOOK, 2001

> The Bible is a window in this prison-world, through which we may look into eternity.

TIMOTHY DWIGHT (1752–1817)
CONGREGATIONALIST MINISTER AND PRESIDENT OF
YALE UNIVERSITY

To most of the prisoners the Bible was entirely new. They listened to it with unfeigned rapture. Mrs. Fry's readings were to them a theatre and a concert, a church and a superior family circle, all rolled into one. Drama and poetry, exciting stories and sublime thoughts, came new and fresh to their ears. The unusual powers of imagination stirred within them. They glimpsed the moving pillar of fire and cloud, they thrilled to the blast of trumpets and the shout that brought down the walls of Jericho, they saw the angels' ladder bright and near, and they touched the hem of the seamless robe whose wearer had shown mercy to a prostitute. In their raw and crude fashion they worshipped, and some of them were profoundly changed.

AN ACCOUNT OF ELIZABETH FRY'S BIBLE READINGS AT
NEWGATE PRISON, LONDON, 1813
QUOTED IN *GOOD NEWS FOR THE WORLD: THE STORY OF
THE BIBLE SOCIETY*, 2004

I know the Bible is inspired because it finds me at
greater depths of my being than any other book.

SAMUEL TAYLOR COLERIDGE (1772–1834)
ENGLISH POET AND LITERARY CRITIC

With the profound divine state whereof I speak,
My mind is stamped more times than once by
evangelic teaching.
This the beginning is; this is the spark which then
dilates into a living flame,
And like a star in heaven shineth in me.

DANTE ALIGHIERI (1265–1321)
ITALIAN POET
"PARADISO" XXIV

I entered the world's great library doors;
I crossed their acres of polished floors;
I searched and searched their stacks and nooks,
And settled at last on the Book of books.

AUTHOR UNKNOWN
QUOTED IN *OUR DAILY BREAD*, MARCH 2004

The New Testament is the very best book that ever
was or will be known in the world.

CHARLES DICKENS (1812–1870)
ENGLISH NOVELIST

Whatever merit there is in anything that I have written is simply due to the fact that when I was a child my mother daily read me a part of the Bible and daily made me learn a part of it by heart.

JOHN RUSKIN (1819-1900)
ENGLISH ART AND SOCIAL CRITIC

Born in the East and clothed in Oriental form and imagery, the Bible walks the ways of all the world with familiar feet and enters land after land to find its own everywhere. It has learned to speak in hundreds of languages to the heart of man. Children listen to its stories with wonder and delight, and wise men ponder them as parables of life. The wicked and the proud tremble at its warnings, but to the wounded and penitent it has a mother's voice. It has woven itself into our dearest dreams; so that Love, Friendship, Sympathy, Devotion, Memory, Hope, put on the beautiful garments of its treasured speech. No man is poor or desolate who has this treasure for his own.

HENRY VAN DYKE
COMPANIONABLE BOOKS, 1922

When the Bible declares that we are made in the "image and likeness" of the Creator, it is affirming that creativity is at our core just as it lies at the core of the Creator of all things.

MATTHEW FOX
EPISCOPALIAN PRIEST AND THEOLOGIAN
CREATIVITY: WHERE THE DIVINE AND HUMAN MEET, 2002

. . . The fact remains that there are things we cannot know. Whatever is happening is simply happening. And, from a spiritual perspective, anything negative that happens has only one purpose: to foster compassion in the human heart. Anything can fuel the fires of compassion if our hearts are open wide enough. As it is written in the Bible, "What man has intended for evil, God intends for good." Even the most horrific situations can increase within us our capacity to love.

MARIANNE WILLIAMSON
EVERYDAY GRACE, 2002

The best commentary on the Bible is the life you lead.

CHURCH SIGN AT THE CHAPEL BY THE SEA
MELBOURNE BEACH, FLORIDA, 2004

All I have done is to put forth, preach and write the Word of God, and apart from this I have done nothing. While I have been sleeping, or drinking Wittenberg beer . . . it is the Word that has done great things. . . . I have done nothing; the Word has done and achieved everything.

MARTIN LUTHER (1485-1546)
GERMAN MONK, THEOLOGIAN AND LEADER OF THE
PROTESTANT REFORMATION

A good man was ther of religioun
And was a poure person of a toun;
But riche he was of hooly thought and werk;
He was also a lerned man, a clerk,
That Cristes Gospel trewley wolde preche:
His parisshens devoutly wolde he teche.

GEOFFREY CHAUCER (C.1340-1400)
ENGLISH POET
PROLOGUE TO *THE CANTERBURY TALES*

Throughout the Bible, a mysterious energy of God pulsates, which, when planted within people, makes for formidable accomplishment.

GORDON MACDONALD
AMERICAN AUTHOR, PASTOR
RENEWING YOUR SPIRITUAL PASSION, 1986

Mine eyes have seen the glory of the coming of the
Lord:
He is trampling out the vintage where the grapes of
wrath are stored;
He hath loosed the fateful lightning of his terrible
swift sword:
His truth is marching on.

I have seen Him in the watch-fires of a hundred
circling camps;
They have builded him an altar in the evening dews
and damps;
I can read His righteous sentence by the dim and
flaring lamps.
His day is marching on.

I have read a fiery gospel, writ in burnished rows of
steel:
"As ye deal with my contemners, so with you my
grace shall deal";
Let the Hero, born of woman, crush the serpent with
his heel,
Since God is marching on.

JULIA WARD HOWE (1819–1910)
AMERICAN CAMPAIGNER FOR WOMEN'S SUFFRAGE AND
ABOLITION OF SLAVERY
"BATTLE-HYMN OF THE REPUBLIC"

This great book, the Bible, this most precious volume
is the heart of God made legible; it is the gold of
God's love, beaten out into gold leaf, so that
therewith our thoughts might be plated, and we also
might have golden, good, and holy thoughts
concerning him.

JOHN BUNYAN (1628-1688)
ENGLISH WRITER AND NONCONFORMIST PREACHER

Without the King James Bible, there would have
been no *Paradise Lost*, no *Pilgrim's Progress*, no
Handel's *Messiah*, no Negro spirituals, and no
Gettysburg Address. These, and innumerable other
works, were inspired by the language of this Bible.
Without this Bible, the culture of the English-
speaking world would have been
immeasurably impoverished.

ALISTER McGRATH
PRINCIPAL OF WYCLIFFE HALL AT OXFORD UNIVERSITY
IN THE BEGINNING: THE STORY OF THE KING JAMES BIBLE, 2001

The Bible, thoroughly known, is literature itself—the
rarest and richest in all departments of thought and
imagination which exists.

JAMES ANTHONY FROUDE (1818-1894)
ENGLISH HISTORIAN AND PROFESSOR

The Bible is an aesthetic achievement, a rendering in verbal form of the interplay of spiritual and material reality, of the Creator and His creation, and in particular of the Creator and His created icon, Man.

GEORGE HOBSON
CANON THEOLOGIAN, AMERICAN CATHEDRAL IN PARIS

As the sun illumines not only the heaven and the whole world, shining on both land and sea; but also sends his rays through windows and small chinks into the furthest recesses of a house; so the Word, poured out everywhere, beholds the smallest actions of human life.

CLEMENT OF ALEXANDRIA (C.150–215)
CHURCH FATHER

To say nothing of its holiness or authority, the Bible contains more specimens of genius and taste than any other volume in existence.

WALTER S. LANDOR (1775–1884)
ENGLISH POET

The Bible is the Book that holds hearts up to the light as if held against the sun.

WILLIAM A. QUAYLE (1860–1925)
METHODIST EPISCOPAL BISHOP AND UNIVERSITY PRESIDENT

Everything that we read in the sacred books shines
and glitters even in the outer shell; but the marrow is
sweeter. He who wants to eat the kernel must
first crack the shell.

ST. JEROME (c.342–420)
DALMATIAN-BORN CHURCH FATHER
(TRANSLATOR OF ORIGINAL-LANGUAGE TEXTS INTO THE
LATIN BIBLE VERSION KNOWN AS *THE VULGATE*)

I have found in the Bible words for my inmost
thoughts, songs for my joy, utterance for my hidden
griefs and pleadings for my shame and feebleness.

SAMUEL TAYLOR COLERIDGE (1772–1834)
ENGLISH POET AND LITERARY CRITIC

Leave not off reading the Bible till you find your
hearts warmed. . . . Let it not only inform you,
but inflame you.

THOMAS WATSON (D.1686)
PURITAN DIVINE

God writes the Gospel not in the Bible alone, but on
trees, and flowers, and clouds, and stars.

MARTIN LUTHER (1485–1546)
GERMAN MONK, THEOLOGIAN AND LEADER OF THE
PROTESTANT REFORMATION

I am thus particularly earnest to display in this work the literary excellence of the Holy Bible, because I have reason to apprehend it is too frequently laid by under a notion of its being a dull, dry and unentertaining system, whereas the fact is quite otherwise: it contains all that can be wished by the truest intellectual taste, it enters more sagaciously and more deeply into human nature, it develops character, delineates manner, charms the imagination and warms the heart more effectively than any other book extant; and if once a man would take it into his hand without that strange prejudicing idea of flatness, and be willing to be pleased, I am morally certain he would find all his favorite authors dwindle in the comparison, and conclude that he was reading not only the most religious book but the most entertaining book in the world.

SAMUEL JACKSON PRATT (1749–1814)
THE SUBLIME AND BEAUTIFUL OF SCRIPTURE, 1777

Then for the style, majestic and divine,
It speaks no less than God in every line.

JOHN DRYDEN (1631–1701)
ENGLISH POET AND DRAMATIST
(ON THE BIBLE)

One must look a long time at the great masterpieces of art to appreciate their beauty and understand their meaning, so one must look a long time at the great verses of the Bible to appreciate their beauty and understand their meaning.

REUBEN ARCHER TORREY (1856-1928)
AMERICAN EVANGELIST, EDUCATOR AND WRITER

Bibles laid open, millions of surprises.

GEORGE HERBERT (1593-1633)
WELSH POET AND PREACHER
THE TEMPLE

Paintings are the Bible of the laity.

JOHANNES GRATIAN (?-C.1179)
ITALIAN MONK AND "FATHER OF CANON LAW"

The Bible is worth all the other books which have ever been printed.

PATRICK HENRY (1736-1799)
AMERICAN STATESMAN AND ORATOR

Every light that comes from Holy Scripture comes from the light of grace.

CATHERINE OF SIENA (1347-1380)
ITALIAN MYSTIC

The Bible is my church. It is always open, and there is my High Priest ever waiting to receive me.

CHARLOTTE ELLIOTT (1789-1871)
ENGLISH HYMN WRITER

"Behold I make all things new." It seemed the one text in the Bible for me that day; for I was walking in a world indescribably beautiful, indescribably lovely.

TEMPLE GAIRDNER (1873-1928)
ENGLISH ANGLICAN MISSIONARY

And we,
syllables of the word,
are uttering Him
who utters the secret of God.

CARYLL HOUSELANDER (1901-1954)
ENGLISH CATHOLIC SPIRITUAL WRITER

The Old and New Testaments are the Great Code of Art.

WILLIAM BLAKE (1757-1827)
BRITISH POET, ARTIST AND MYSTIC

It is a great thing, this reading of Scriptures! For it is not possible to ever exhaust the mind of the Scriptures. It is a well that has no bottom.

JOHN CHRYSOSTOM (C.347–407)
ARCHBISHOP OF CONSTANTINOPLE AND CHURCH FATHER

The English Bible, a book which, if everything else in our language should perish, would alone suffice to show the whole extent of its beauty and power.

THOMAS BABINGTON (LORD MACAULAY) (1800–1859)
ON JOHN DRYDEN, 1828

Within that aweful volume lies
The mystery of mysteries!
Happiest they of human race,
To whom our God has granted grace
To read, to fear, to hope, to pray,
To lift the latch and force the way:
And better had they ne'er been born,
Who read to doubt or read to scorn.

SIR WALTER SCOTT (1771–1832)
SCOTTISH NOVELIST
"THE MONASTERY"

In the Old Testament the New is concealed, in the New Testament the Old is revealed.

ST. AUGUSTINE OF HIPPO (354–430)
DOCTOR OF THE CHURCH AND PHILOSOPHER

There is one Book, and only one, which embraces all the heights and depths of human nature. The Bible belongs to those elemental things—like the sky and the wind and the sea, like bread and wine, like the kisses of little children and tears shed beside the grave—which can never grow stale or out of date, because they are the common heritage of mankind.

T. H. DARLOW (THOMAS HERBERT DARLOW)
(1858–1927)
CONGREGATIONALIST THEOLOGIAN AND BIBLE SCHOLAR
THE GREATEST BOOK IN THE WORLD, 1927

The Bible tells a story . . . The story of salvation runs like a golden thread through everything else that the Bible contains, whether songs, prayers, contemplation and wisdom, theological knowledge and priestly service, law, praise, experience of liturgy. It is this thread that matters, that gives firmness and design to everything else.

NETHERLANDS REFORMED CHURCH
THE BIBLE SPEAKS AGAIN, 1969

Holy Bible, Book divine,
Precious treasure, thou art mine;
Mine to teach me whence I came;
Mine to teach me what I am.

Mine to chide me when I rove;
Mine to show a Savior's love;
Mine thou art to guide and guard;
Mine to punish or reward.

Mine to comfort in distress,
Suff'ring in this wilderness;
Mine to show, by living faith,
Men can triumph over death.

Mine to tell of joys to come,
And the rebel sinner's doom;
O Thou Holy Book divine,
Precious treasure, thou art mine.
Amen.

JOHN BURTON SR. (1773–1822)
ENGLISH BAPTIST LAYMAN
HYMN, "HOLY BIBLE, BOOK DIVINE"

I must confess to you that the majesty of the
Scriptures astonishes me. . . .

JEAN-JACQUES ROUSSEAU (1712–1778)
FRENCH PHILOSOPHER AND NOVELIST

Do more beloved words exist? Framed and hung in
hospital halls, scratched on prison walls, quoted by
the young, and whispered by the dying. In these lines
sailors have found a harbor, the frightened have
found a father, and strugglers have found a friend.
And because the passage is so deeply loved, it is
widely known. Can you find ears on which these
words have never fallen? Set to music in a hundred
songs, translated into a thousand tongues, domiciled
in a million hearts. One of those hearts
might be yours.

MAX LUCADO
AMERICAN PASTOR AND AUTHOR
TRAVELING LIGHT, 2001
(ON PSALM 23, "THE LORD IS MY SHEPHERD...")

The Bible grows more beautiful, as we grow in our
understanding of it.

JOHANN WOLFGANG VON GOETHE (1749–1832)
GERMAN POET AND NOVELIST

The greatest source of material for motion pictures is
the Bible, and almost any chapter in the Bible would
serve as a basic idea for a motion picture.

CECIL B. DE MILLE (1881–1959)
AMERICAN FILM PRODUCER AND DIRECTOR

You do well not to let drop from your hands the polished mirror of the holy Gospel of your Lord, for it provides the likeness of everyone who looks into it. . . . There the kingdom of heaven is depicted, visible to those who have a luminous eye.

EPHRAEM THE SYRIAN (C.303-373)
CHURCH FATHER AND SPIRITUAL WRITER

God chose to use human effort and inclination, and earthly disciplines of writing and recording, as he chooses to use all worthy human work. He took the biblical author's skills, sanctified them, and used them for this glory in the transmission of his Word to future generations, including us.

ISABEL SANDERS THROOP
AMERICAN WRITER

If we Christians wish to understand the psalms, we must bear in mind that the roots of their thought lie in the past, in the Old Testament, while their blossoming reaches out into the far future, to the end of the world, to heaven itself.

PIUS DRIJVERS
DUTCH THEOLOGIAN
THE PSALMS: THEIR STRUCTURE AND MEANING, 1965

By reading the scriptures I am so renewed that all
nature seems renewed around me and with me. The
sky seems to be a pure, a cooler blue, the trees a
deeper green, light is sharper on the outlines of the
forest and the hills. The whole world is charged with
the glory of God and I feel fire and music . . .
under my feet.

THOMAS MERTON (1915–1968)
FRENCH-BORN TRAPPIST MONK AND POET
THOUGHTS IN SOLITUDE, 1958

The mystery of the Bible should teach us, at one and
the same time, our nothingness and our greatness,
producing humility and animating hope.

HENRY MELVILLE (1819–1891)
AMERICAN NOVELIST AND POET

———◦•◦◦•◦———

Then he opened their minds so they could understand the Scriptures. . . .

While he was blessing them, he left them and was taken up
into heaven.

LUKE 24:45, 51

The POWER of the BIBLE to
SHAPE
CIVILIZATIONS

𝒯hen Jesus came to them and said, "All authority in heaven and on earth has been given to me. Therefore go and make disciples of all nations, baptizing them in the name of the Father and of the Son and of the Holy Spirit, and teaching them to obey everything I have commanded you. And surely I am with you always, to the very end of the age."

MATTHEW 28:18–20
THE GREAT COMMISSION

England has two books, the Bible and Shakespeare.
England made Shakespeare, but the Bible
made England.

VICTOR HUGO (1802–1885)
FRENCH POET AND NOVELIST

This Bible is for the Government of the People, by the People, and for the People.

JOHN WYCLIFFE (1320–1384)
ENGLISH REFORMER AND BIBLE TRANSLATOR

For nearly four hundred years, and throughout several revisions of its English form, the King James Bible has been deeply revered among the English-speaking peoples of the world. The precision of translation for which it is historically renowned, and its majesty of style, have enabled that monumental version of the Word of God to become the mainspring of the religion, language, and legal foundations of our civilization.

MY UTMOST DEVOTIONAL BIBLE
PREFACE, 1992

We present you with this Book, the most valuable thing that this world affords. Here is wisdom; this is the Royal Law; these are the lively Oracles of God.

CORONATION SERVICE FOR THE NEW BRITISH MONARCH
PRESENTATION OF THE HOLY BIBLE, 1689

We have a social gospel. We need a systematic theology large enough to match it and vital enough to back it.

WALTER RAUSCHENBUSCH (1861–1918)
AMERICAN PACIFIST

The Lord has more light and truth yet to break forth out of his holy word.

JOHN ROBINSON (1576–1625)
ENGLISH PASTOR
(ADDRESS TO THE DEPARTING PILGRIMS, 1620)

It is the best gift God has given to men. All the good Savior gave to the world was communicated through this book. But for it we could not know right from wrong. All things desirable for man's welfare, here and hereafter, are to be found portrayed in it.

ABRAHAM LINCOLN (1809–1865)
PRESIDENT OF THE UNITED STATES
(REPLY TO A COMMITTEE PRESENTING A BIBLE)

Abraham Lincoln used scripture quotations very frequently and very powerfully. Probably no Bible quotation, or, for that matter, no quotation from any book ever has had more influence upon people than the famous quotation made by Lincoln in his

Springfield (Ill.) speech of 1812—"A house divided against itself cannot stand." It is said that he had searched for some time for a phrase which would present in the strongest possible way the proposition he intended to advance—namely, that the nation could not endure half-slave and half-free.

WILLIAM JENNINGS BRYAN (1860-1925)
DEMOCRATIC POLITICIAN AND POPULIST

Throughout the history of the western world, the Scriptures, Jewish and Christian, have been the great instigators of the revolt against the worst forms of clerical and political despotism. The Bible has been the *Magna Carta* of the poor and of the oppressed.

THOMAS H. HUXLEY (1825-1895)
BRITISH BIOLOGIST

I would say here something that was heard from an ecclesiastic of the most eminent degree: "That the intention of the Holy Ghost is to teach us how one goes to heaven, not how the heavens go."

GALILEO GALILEI (1564-1642)
ITALIAN SCIENTIST
(DEFENDING CHARGES THAT HIS ASTRONOMICAL THEORIES
SEEMED TO CONFLICT WITH THE BIBLE)

The old, for the English, is holy and beautiful, largely because the language of the King James Bible has conveyed that to them.

ADAM NICHOLSON
GOD'S SECRETARIES: THE MAKING OF THE KING JAMES BIBLE, 2003

Don't give up! Don't get discouraged! I have read the end of the book! We win!

DESMOND TUTU
ARCHBISHOP OF CAPETOWN AND CIVIL RIGHTS ACTIVIST

The existence of the Bible, as a book for the people, is the greatest benefit which the human race has ever experienced. Every attempt to belittle it is a crime against humanity.

IMMANUEL KANT (1724–1804)
GERMAN PHILOSOPHER

It is impossible to mentally or socially enslave a Bible-reading people. The principles of the Bible are the groundwork of human freedom.

HORACE GREELEY (1811–1872)
FOUNDER AND EDITOR OF THE *NEW YORK TRIBUNE*

The general diffusion of the Bible is the most effectual way to civilize and humanize mankind; to purify and exalt the general system of public morals; to give efficacy to the just precepts of international and municipal law; to enforce the observance of prudence, temperance, justice and fortitude; and to improve all the relations of social and domestic life.

JAMES KENT (1763-1847)
AMERICAN JURIST

The Gospel is not merely a book—it is a living power—a book surpassing all others. I never omit to read it, and every day with the same pleasure. Nowhere is to be found such a series of beautiful ideas, and admirable moral maxims, which pass before us like the battalions of a celestial army. . . . The soul can never go astray with this book for its guide.

NAPOLEON BONAPARTE (1769-1821)
FRENCH GENERAL AND EMPEROR

The reverence for the Scriptures is an element of civilization, for thus has the history of the world been preserved, and is preserved.

RALPH WALDO EMERSON (1803-1882)
AMERICAN ESSAYIST, POET AND PHILOSOPHER

The first question ever asked by an Inquisitor of a
"heretic" was whether he knew any part of the
Bible in his own tongue. It was asked in 1233 of a
man who belonged to a dissident religious sect
known as the Waldensians, which emphasized Bible
study and lay preaching; it would be asked again of
thousands of others before the course of history
would render its dark implications null and void.

BENSON BOBRICK
THE MAKING OF THE ENGLISH BIBLE, 2001

I have an implicit faith . . . that mankind can only be
saved through non-violence, which is the central
teaching of the Bible, as I have understood the Bible.

MAHATMA GANDHI (MOHANDAS KARAMCHAND
GANDHI) (1869-1948)
INDIAN STATESMAN AND PACIFIST

To this day the common Britisher or citizen of the
United States of North America accepts and
worships it as a single book by a single author, the
book being the Book of Books and the
author being God.

GEORGE BERNARD SHAW (1856-1950)
IRISH DRAMATIST

To all serving in my Forces by sea, or land, or in the air, and indeed to all my people engaged in the defence of the Realm, I commend the reading of this book. For centuries the Bible has been a wholesome and strengthening influence in our national life, and it behoves us in these momentous days to turn with renewed faith to this Divine source of comfort and inspiration.

KING GEORGE VI (1895-1952)
KING OF GREAT BRITAIN AND NORTHERN IRELAND
FROM 1936
(MESSAGE PRINTED IN POCKET-SIZED NEW TESTAMENTS
DISTRIBUTED TO THE BRITISH ARMED FORCES DURING
WORLD WAR II)

There never was found, in any age of the world, either religion or law that did so highly exalt the public good as the Bible.

SIR FRANCIS BACON (1561-1626)
ENGLISH LAWYER, PHILOSOPHER AND ESSAYIST

There are no songs comparable to the songs of Zion; no orations equal to those of the prophets; no politics like those which the Scriptures teach.

JOHN MILTON (1608-1674)
ENGLISH POET, AUTHOR OF *PARADISE LOST*

Without the Bible we would never have known the abolitionist movement, the prison-reform movement, the anti-war movement, the labor movement, the civil rights movement, the movement of indigenous and dispossessed peoples for their human rights, the anti-apartheid movement in South Africa, the Solidarity movement in Poland, the free-speech and pro-democracy movements in such Far Eastern countries as South Korea, the Philippines, and even China. These movements of modern times have all employed the language of the Bible.

THOMAS CAHILL
THE GIFTS OF THE JEWS: HOW A TRIBE OF DESERT NOMADS CHANGED THE WAY EVERYONE THINKS AND FEELS, 1998

"Where are we today?" That is the question uppermost in the minds of many people as they approach a study of Bible prophecy in general and of the book of Revelation in particular. They instinctively feel that the Bible should speak clearly to the special needs of our age. They are right: it should, and it does.

JOHN PHILLIPS
BRITISH BIBLE SCHOLAR
EXPLORING REVELATION, 1987

If we abide by the principles taught in the Bible, our country will go on prospering and to prosper; but if we and our posterity neglect its instructions and authority, no man can tell how sudden a catastrophe may overwhelm us and bury all our glory in profound obscurity.

DANIEL WEBSTER (1782–1852)
AMERICAN STATESMAN, LAWYER AND ORATOR

We believe that it is the best source of information or wisdom available to human kind concerning the most important issues of life. Actually it is unique; whatever part of the church we come from, this is what we should grasp. Public and private matters are always tightly intertwined with these "matters of life." And that's why the witness of Scripture concerning them needs to be heard clearly in our day.

JAMES CATFORD
BRITISH CHIEF EXECUTIVE OF THE BIBLE SOCIETY

It was a common saying among the Puritans "Brown bread and the Gospel is good fare."

MATTHEW HENRY (1662–1714)
ENGLISH BIBLE COMMENTATOR

... It is one thing to appreciate the praises of great men who have valued the Bible and quite another to recognise its relevance to ourselves and to our day.

CYRIL BULLEY
ANGLICAN BISHOP AND FORMER CHAPLAIN TO HER MAJESTY
THE QUEEN
GLIMPSES OF THE DIVINE, 1987

Mark is said to have been the first man to set out for Egypt and preach there the gospel which he had himself written down, and the first to establish churches in Alexandria itself.

EUSEBIUS OF CAESAREA (C. 260-341)
THEOLOGIAN AND "FATHER OF CHURCH HISTORY"

About the one hundred and fiftieth year after the coming of the English to Britain, Pope Gregory was inspired by God to send his servant Augustine with several other God-fearing monks to preach the word of God to the English nation.

THE VENERABLE BEDE (673-735)
ENGLISH HISTORIAN, SCHOLAR AND MONK OF JARROW
A HISTORY OF THE ENGLISH CHURCH AND PEOPLE,
EIGHTH CENTURY

If God spare my life, ere many years, I will cause a boy that driveth the plough shall know more of the scriptures than thou doest.

WILLIAM TYNDALE (C.1492-1536)
BIBLE SCHOLAR, TRANSLATOR AND "FATHER OF
THE ENGLISH BIBLE"
(IN AN ARGUMENT WITH A PRIEST EXASPERATED BY HIS
INSISTENCE ON SCRIPTURAL AUTHORITY)

As long as there are human rights to be defended; as long as there are great interests to be guarded; as long as the welfare of nations is a matter for discussion, so long will public speaking have its place. By far the most useful quotations for an orator . . . are those from Holy Writ. The people are more familiar with the Bible than with any other single book, and lessons drawn from it reinforce a speech.

WILLIAM JENNINGS BRYAN (1860-1925)
DEMOCRATIC POLITICIAN AND POPULIST

The English Bible is the first of our national treasures.

KING GEORGE V (1865-1936)
KING OF GREAT BRITAIN AND IRELAND FROM 1910

God suffers in the multitude of souls that His holy
Word cannot reach. Religious truth is imprisoned in
a small number of manuscript books, which confine
instead of spreading the public treasure.
Yes, it is a press, certainly, but a press from which
shall soon flow, in inexhaustible streams, the most
abundant and most marvelous refreshment that has
ever flowed to relieve the thirst of men. Through it,
God will spread His Word. A spring of pure truth
shall flow from it; like a new star of hope it shall
scatter the darkness of ignorance and cause a light
heretofore unknown to shine amongst men.

JOHANN GUTENBERG (C. 1399–1498)
GERMAN INVENTOR OF MOVEABLE TYPES IN PRINTING

You can speak to academics, archaeologists,
theologians, psychologists, priests, monks, nuns,
missionaries, even Islamic scholars or Jewish rabbis,
who will tell you that the Bible is the most important
collection of documents in the world. You can speak
to ordinary Christians who will tell you that it is a
book which has changed their lives.

ROGER STEER
GOOD NEWS FOR THE WORLD: THE STORY OF
THE BIBLE SOCIETY, 2004

Next to the Bible itself, the English Bible was (and is) the most influential book ever published. It gave every literate person complete access to the sacred text, which helped to foster the spirit of inquiry through reading and reflection. These in turn accelerated the growth of commercial printing and the ever-widening circulation and production of books. . . . Once the people were free to interpret the Word of God according to the light of their own understanding, they began to question the authority of their inherited institutions, both religious and secular, which led to reformation within the Church, and to the rise of constitutional government in England and the end of the divine right of kings.

BENSON BOBRICK
THE MAKING OF THE ENGLISH BIBLE, 2001

I have a great mind to found a policy upon the Bible, in public life observing the strictest justice, and not only cold justice, but active benevolence.

ANTHONY ASHLEY COOPER (LATER THE EARL OF
SHAFTESBURY) (1801–1885)
BRITISH MEMBER OF PARLIAMENT, SOCIAL REFORMER
AND EVANGELIST
(JOURNAL ENTRY WHILE A STUDENT AT HARROW)

I have found my destiny. I must take the gospel to the people of the East End.

WILLIAM BOOTH (1829-1912)
FOUNDER OF THE SALVATION ARMY
(REFERRING TO THE SQUALID SECTION OF LONDON)

Give me a candle and a Bible, and shut me up in a dark dungeon, and I will tell you what the whole world is doing.

AUTHOR UNKNOWN
QUOTED IN *THE NEW ENCYCLOPEDIA OF CHRISTIAN QUOTATIONS*, 2000

Talk about the questions of the day; there is but one question, and that is the gospel. It can and will correct everything needing correction.

WILLIAM EWART GLADSTONE (1809-1898)
PRIME MINISTER OF GREAT BRITAIN

For the Christian people there are no people beyond the power of God's word. Christians know no "barbarians," but only strangers whom we hope to make our friends.

STANLEY HAUERWAS
AMERICAN PROFESSOR OF THEOLOGICAL ETHICS

Then Doug suggested that we pray together at my desk. At first I was concerned what my partners would think if one of them burst through the door. But Doug was so natural and relaxed that I relaxed, too. He thanked the Lord for bringing us together in the bonds of fellowship, for letting us know His love. I stumbled and stammered through my prayer; it was the first time I had prayed aloud with anyone in my life.

My new friend then handed me a copy of the Phillips version of the New Testament, inscribed: *To Charles—It is better to fail in a cause that will ultimately succeed than to succeed in a cause that will ultimately fail—God bless you! Doug. Matthew 6:33.* How those words were to haunt and then lead me in the days to come!

CHARLES W. COLSON
FORMER WHITE HOUSE COUNSEL AND FOUNDER OF
PRISON FELLOWSHIP
BORN AGAIN, 1972
(ACCOUNT OF HIS RELIGIOUS CONVERSION DURING THE
WATERGATE INVESTIGATION)

That book accounts for the supremacy of England.

QUEEN VICTORIA (1819–1901)
LONGEST-REIGNING BRITISH MONARCH

No Greater Moral Change ever passed over a nation
than passed over England in the latter part of the
reign of Queen Elizabeth. England became the people
of a Book, and That Book Was The Bible. It was
Read by Every Class of People. And the Effect was
Amazing. The Whole Moral Tone of the
Nation was Changed.

JOHN RICHARD GREEN (1837–1883)
A SHORT HISTORY OF THE ENGLISH PEOPLE, 1874

. . . The religious face of Europe was being
transfigured by the Bible—by lectures, disputations,
and commentaries still in the Latin of the
international academy and the religious professionals,
by sermons and catechizing in the language of the
populace, by public debates between opposing
authorities in front of citizen assemblies called to
vote for or against the new biblical gospel, by
placards, posters, woodcuts, and cartoons, by
vernacular service-books and liturgical lections and
numerous other media of the open Bible.

THE OXFORD ILLUSTRATED HISTORY OF THE BIBLE, 2001
(ON THE PERIOD FROM THE REFORMATION TO 1700)

The whole hope of human progress is suspended on the ever growing influence of the Bible.

W. H. SEWARD (1801–1872)
AMERICAN POLITICIAN

It is impossible to rightly govern the world without God and the Bible.

GEORGE WASHINGTON (1732–1799)
FIRST PRESIDENT OF THE UNITED STATES OF AMERICA

The ability of the biblical record to put on trial the whole of its own culture, to examine with shocking honesty its failures, that historical quest and presentation is in itself a tribute to the influence of the prophetic quest to see the world of the everyday through the eyes of an eternal God.

JONATHAN MAGONET
A RABBI'S BIBLE, 1991

The gospel gives us different priorities from those of the popular culture and offers us a different agenda from that of the political economy.

JIM WALLIS
SPEAKER, ACTIVIST AND FOUNDER OF THE
SOJOURNERS COMMUNITY

What I began to see was that the Bible is not essentially, as I had always more or less supposed, a book of ethical principles, of moral exhortations, of cautionary tales about exemplary people, of uplifting thoughts—in fact, not really a religious book at all . . . I saw it instead as a great, tattered compendium of writings, the underlying and unifying purpose of all of which is to show how God works through the Jacobs and Jabboks of history to make himself known to the world and to draw the world back to himself.

FREDERICK BUECHNER
AWARD-WINNING AUTHOR AND CHRISTIAN APOLOGIST
NOW AND THEN, 1983

Scripture isn't meant as scientific exposition or as mere history. It is "salvation history," a spiritual drama of an overarching compassion and concern for human integrity, of an unwavering love that seeks an answering affirmation. It is a vivid, sometimes parabolic account of God's persistent, unrelenting quest for us and our stumbling, often faithless response.

GEORGE W. CORNELL
THE UNTAMED GOD, 1975

The Bible also wonderfully seems to be what it claims to be. Its underlying unity of theme is the more impressive because it is a library of sixty-six books written by some forty authors over about fifteen hundred years. Its Old Testament prophecies were remarkably fulfilled. Its doctrines are profound and its ethics noble. Nearly two thousand years after Christ its popularity continues to increase. It has brought forgiveness to the guilty, freedom to the oppressed, guidance to the perplexed, consolation to the dying, and hope to the bereaved. Everyone who reads it with an open mind and a humble spirit testifies to its power to disturb and to comfort.

JOHN R. W. STOTT
RECTOR EMERITUS OF ALL SOULS CHURCH, LONDON
CHRISTIAN BASICS: BEGINNINGS, BELIEFS, AND BEHAVIOR, 1991

So great is my veneration for the Bible that the earlier my children begin to read it, the more confident will be my hope that they will prove useful citizens to their country, and respectable members of society.

JOHN QUINCY ADAMS (1767-1848)
PRESIDENT OF THE UNITED STATES OF AMERICA

Because the Bible is *God's Word*, it has *eternal relevance*; it speaks to all humankind, in every age and in every culture. Because it is God's Word, we must listen—and obey. But because God chose to speak his Word through *human words in history*, every book in the Bible also has *historical particularity*; each document is conditioned by the language, time and culture in which it was originally written . . . Interpretation of the Bible is demanded by the "tension" that exists between its *eternal relevance* and its *historical particularity*.

GORDON D. FEE AND DOUGLAS STUART
HOW TO READ THE BIBLE FOR ALL ITS WORTH, 1981

Through his action in history, God is known to be engaged in a dramatic struggle with the powers which are responsible for this world's darkness. . . . The acts, the purpose and the demands of the Lord of history, together with the nature, task and life of the new community which he has brought into being as a foretaste of society's goal—these constitute the Bible's central content to which all its teachings are subsidiary.

G. ERNEST WRIGHT
THE BIBLICAL DOCTRINE OF MAN IN SOCIETY, 1954

The Bible has a sense of direction all its own. It is not a map of the journey from Eden to Armageddon, it is the journey.

BRIAN REDHEAD AND FRANCES GUMLEY
THE GOOD BOOK, 1987

Any one who's not prepared to listen to God in the first place has nothing to say to the world.

HANS URS VON BALTHASAR (1905–1988)
SWISS ROMAN CATHOLIC THEOLOGIAN

The Bible is the supreme source document of Christianity but it is not the private property of Christians. It has a power and a pertinence for people of every kind and in every age. It speaks about God but it also speaks from God and concerns itself with the struggles, tragedies, aspirations and destinies of humanity itself. This has given it a contemporary relevance across the centuries and enabled it to be a light on the journey of life for all humankind.

ROY WILLIAMSON
BISHOP OF SOUTHWARK
FOREWORD TO *MY WORD*, 2002

We cannot segregate God's word from the historical
reality in which it is proclaimed. It would not then
be God's word. It would be history, it would be a
pious book, a Bible that is just a book in our library.
It becomes God's word because it verifies,
enlightens, contrasts, repudiates, praises what is
going on today in this society.

OSCAR ROMERO (1917–1980)
CATHOLIC ARCHBISHOP OF EL SALVADOR
(ASSASSINATED FOR SPEAKING OUT AGAINST
THE MILITARY REGIME)

The Bible is the greatest traveler in the world. It
penetrates into every country, civilized and
uncivilized. It is seen in the royal palace and in the
humble cottage. It is the friend of emperors and
beggars. It is read by the light of the dim candle
amid Arctic snows. It is read under the glare of the
equatorial sun. It is read in city and country, amid
the crowds and in solitude. Wherever the message is
received, it frees the mind from bondage and
fills the heart with gladness.

ARTHUR T. PIERSON (1837–1911)
AMERICAN PRESBYTERIAN MINISTER

The Western world has let itself be profoundly inspired by the biblical traditions, which have penetrated right down to the fundamental ideas and values of modern times. In the biblical story of God, it found again its own history of freedom, and it has continued to identify itself with that history, even in its now secular forms.

JURGEN MOLTMANN
GERMAN PROFESSOR OF SYSTEMATIC THEOLOGY
GOD FOR A SECULAR SOCIETY, 1999

In Belmarsh Prison we get through thousands of Bibles as all the prisoners want to read the Scriptures and God has been so good in bringing so many to himself. I always show this passage from Genesis to the prisoners to remind them that God will be with them in Belmarsh, that is if they want him to be. We now have to provide the Bible in forty different languages, ranging from Persian to Chinese and Urdu.

DAVID POWE
SENIOR CHAPLAIN AT HER MAJESTY'S PRISON, BELMARSH
(REFERRING TO GENESIS 39:20-21, "BUT WHILE JOSEPH WAS
THERE IN THE PRISON, THE LORD WAS WITH HIM; HE
SHOWED HIM KINDNESS AND GRANTED HIM FAVOR IN THE
EYES OF THE PRISON WARDEN.")

It is a thing plainly repugnant to the Word of God,
and the custom of the Primitive Church, to have
publick prayer in the Church, or to minister the
Sacraments in a tongue not understanded
of the people.

ARTICLES OF RELIGION
THE BOOK OF COMMON PRAYER, 1562

Hold fast to the Bible as the sheet-anchor of your
liberties; write its precepts in your hearts and
practice them in your lives. To the influence of this
book we are indebted for all the progress made in
true civilization, and to this we must look as
our guide in the future.

ULYSSES S. GRANT (1822-1885)
PRESIDENT OF THE UNITED STATES OF AMERICA

Nor can the Bible be closed until the last
great man is born.

RALPH WALDO EMERSON (1803-1882)
AMERICAN PHILOSOPHER, POET AND ESSAYIST
REPRESENTATIVE MEN: USES OF GREAT MEN, 1850

The Gospel of Christ knows of no religion but social;
no holiness but social holiness.

JOHN WESLEY (1703–1791)
ENGLISH PREACHER AND FOUNDER OF METHODISM

Just as it does in proclaiming the truths of faith, and
even more so in presenting the foundations and
content of Christian morality, the new evangelization
will show its authenticity and unleash all its
missionary force when it is carried out through the
gift not only of the word proclaimed but also of
the word lived.

POPE JOHN PAUL II (1920–2005)
POLISH PRIEST AND PHILOSOPHER
ENCYCLICAL LETTER *VERITATIS SPLENDOR*, 1993

The principles of Christianity, deeply engraved on
the heart, would be infinitely more powerful than
the false honour of monarchies, than the humane
virtues of republics, or the servile fear
of despotic states.

MONTESQUIEU (CHARLES-LOUIS DE SECONDAT)
(1689–1755)
FRENCH POLITICAL PHILOSOPHER
SPIRIT OF LAWS, 1748

For more than a thousand years the Bible, collectively taken, has gone hand in hand with civilization, science, law—in short, with the moral and intellectual cultivation of the species, always supporting and often leading the way.

SAMUEL TAYLOR COLERIDGE (1772–1834)
ENGLISH POET AND LITERARY CRITIC

A Bible and a newspaper in every house, a good school in every district—all studied and appreciated as they merit—are the principal support of virtue, morality, and civil liberty.

BENJAMIN FRANKLIN (1706–1790)
AMERICAN STATESMAN, INVENTOR AND SCIENTIST

The Bible is one of the greatest blessings bestowed by God on the children of men. It has God for its author, salvation for its end, and truth without any mixture for its matter. It is all pure, all sincere; nothing too much, nothing wanting.

JOHN LOCKE (1632–1704)
ENGLISH PHILOSOPHER AND POLITICAL THEORIST

The Bible has always been regarded as part of the common law of England.

SIR WILLIAM BLACKSTONE (1723–1780)
ENGLISH JURIST
COMMENTARIES ON THE LAWS OF ENGLAND, 1765–1769

To call the Bible a great book is an understatement. It is, quite simply, the cornerstone of Western Civilization. In its two testaments, it stands as law and scripture for two of the great religions of the world. And it shares with a third, the Muslim faith, several of its significant figures and stories. But the Bible's reach extends beyond the realm of religion. As a work of literature, it has had an immeasurable impact on our greatest writers, artists and composers—and thus, on our culture as a whole. Directly and indirectly, it has shaped our ideas about good and evil, loyalty and betrayal, hope and despair, love and hate, and the meaning of life itself.

CHARLTON HESTON PRESENTS THE BIBLE, 1997

O earth, earth, earth, hear the word of the Lord.

JEREMIAH 22:29 KJV

The POWER of the BIBLE to
ENDURE
CHALLENGES

Then Jesus said to them, "Don't you understand this parable? How then will you understand any parable? The farmer sows the word. Some people are like seed along the path, where the word is sown. As soon as they hear it, Satan comes and takes away the word that was sown in them. Others, like seed sown on rocky places, hear the word and at once receive it with joy. But since they have no root, they last only a short time. When trouble or persecution comes because of the word, they quickly fall away. Still others, like seed sown among thorns, hear the word; but the worries of this life, the deceitfulness of wealth and the desires for other things come in and choke the word, making it unfruitful. Others, like seed sown on good soil, hear the word, accept it, and produce a crop—thirty, sixty or even a hundred times what was sown."

MARK 4:13-20
THE PARABLE OF THE SOWER

The devil can cite Scripture for his purpose.

WILLIAM SHAKESPEARE (1564–1616)
ENGLISH DRAMATIST
THE MERCHANT OF VENICE

Cities fall, empires come to nothing, kingdoms fade away as smoke . . . But that this book no tyrant should have been able to consume, no tradition to choke, no heretic maliciously to corrupt; that it should stand unto this day, amid the wreck of all that was human, without the alteration of one sentence so as to change the doctrine taught therein—surely there is a very singular providence, claiming our attention in a most remarkable manner.

JOHN JEWELL (1522–1571)
ENGLISH BISHOP AND PURITAN LEADER

Even if a thousand trumpets were to sound in the ears of the dead, they would never hear them. That is how it is with a soul . . . that has lost all memory of God, a soul that never thinks of God all day: it does not hear that sound of the Word that is calling it.

PHILOXENUS OF MABBUG (c.440–523)
SYRIAN BISHOP, SAINT AND THEOLOGIAN

No women, prentices, journeymen, servingmen, husbandmen nor labourers shall read the Bible.

DECREED IN ENGLAND, 1543

CHRISTIAN, *n.* One who believes that the New Testament is a divinely inspired book admirably suited to the spiritual needs of his neighbor.

AMBROSE BIERCE (1842–1914)
AMERICAN JOURNALIST AND SATIRIST
THE DEVIL'S DICTIONARY, 1911

The pernicious habit of quoting proof-texts—often to support our own point of view—dies hard. You can prove anything you want to by taking a text out of context, or by conveniently forgetting another passage which gives a different slant on the matter. If we want to know what Jesus taught on a particular subject, we must patiently try to find *all* he said about it. . . . Above all we must remember that all his teaching was linked to one all-embracing theme—the gospel he preached.

A. GORDON JONES
WHAT DID JESUS TEACH? 1969

The truth is, their opinions on the subject of religion are not formed from the perusal of the Word of God. The Bible lies on the shelf unopened; and they would be wholly ignorant of its contents, except for what they hear occasionally at church, or for the faint traces which their memories may still retain of the lessons of their earliest infancy.
. . . When God of His goodness hath vouchsafed to grant us such abundant means of instruction in that which we are most concerned to know, how great must be the guilt, and how awful the punishment, of voluntary ignorance!

WILLIAM WILBERFORCE (1759–1833)
BRITISH MEMBER OF PARLIAMENT, ABOLITIONIST AND
EVANGELICAL LEADER
*A PRACTICAL VIEW OF THE PREVAILING RELIGIOUS SYSTEM OF
PROFESSED CHRISTIANS*, 1797

Wise and learned religious men interpret the great heart of God not by their own hearts but by their intellects . . . They are the slaves of the letter in all its weaknesses and imperfections—and will be until the Spirit and the Word, the Spirit of obedience, shall set them free.

GEORGE MACDONALD (1824–1905)
SCOTTISH NOVELIST, POET AND PASTOR

This court acknowledges, as I suppose, the validity of the law of God. I see a book kissed here which I suppose to be the Bible, or at least the New Testament. That teaches me that all things whatsoever I would that men should do unto me, I should do even so unto them. It teaches me, further, to "remember them that are in bonds, as bound with them." I endeavored to act upon that instruction . . . Now, if it is deemed necessary that I should forfeit my life for the furtherance of the ends of justice, and mingle my blood further with the blood of my children and with the blood of millions in this slave country whose rights are disregarded by wicked, cruel and unjust enactments—I submit; so let it be done!

JOHN BROWN (1800–1859)
AMERICAN ABOLITIONIST
(LAST SPEECH TO THE COURT BEFORE HIS EXECUTION
FOR INSURRECTION)

The Bible tells us to love our neighbours, and also to love our enemies; probably because they are generally the same people.

G. K. CHESTERTON (GILBERT KEITH CHESTERTON)
(1874–1936)
ENGLISH ESSAYIST, NOVELIST AND POET

Perhaps the most disturbing factor in the whole question of the modern attitude to the Bible is that all of us, inside and outside the Church, young and old, believers and agnostics, share to some extent the temper of the age we live in. None of us can remain untouched by the various undercurrents of contemporary thought. We all have part in the general perplexity and confusion of mind. For some it is offset by ingrained religious habits, for others by personal religious experience which is impervious to doubt. For most of us, however, the position is rather that we are at a loss to know what to make of the Bible. We should welcome some reassurance that it has not disintegrated under the impact of the modern world and that it still stands unimpaired, a rock among shifting sands.

WILLIAM NEIL
THE REDISCOVERY OF THE BIBLE, 1954

The Scripture in time of disputes is like an open town in time of war, which serves indifferently the occasions of both parties.

ALEXANDER POPE (1688–1744)
ENGLISH POET
THOUGHTS ON VARIOUS SUBJECTS, 1727

I fear that the gospel has suffered more damage from clever men than from anything else.

CHARLES HADDON SPURGEON (1834–1892)
ENGLISH NONCONFORMIST PREACHER
(REPUTED TO BE ONE OF THE GREATEST PREACHERS
OF ALL TIME)

We may well feel alarmed and sorry that the habit of simple and disciplined Bible-reading has so largely disappeared from Christian homes . . . What we have now is, on the one hand, numbers of people who though they are believing Christians never open their Bibles even in church; and on the other, the devoted few who wrestle with the Scriptures with the help of commentaries learned or popular, whose chief effect is to show them what difficulties they are up against.

ERIK ROUTLEY
THE WISDOM OF THE FATHERS, 1957

Voltaire expected that within fifty years of his lifetime there would not be one Bible in the world. Today, his house is a distribution center for Bibles in many languages.

CORRIE TEN BOOM (1892–1983)
WRITER, SPEAKER AND CONCENTRATION CAMP SURVIVOR

The word unto the prophet spoken
Was writ on tablets yet unbroken;
The word by seers or sibyls told,
In groves of oak, or fanes of gold,
Still floats upon the morning wind,
Still whispers to the willing mind.
One accent of the Holy Ghost
The heedless world hath never lost.

RALPH WALDO EMERSON (1803-1882)
AMERICAN ESSAYIST, POET AND PHILOSOPHER
"THE PROBLEM"

We fail in our duty to study God's Word not so much because it is difficult to understand, not so much because it is dull and boring, but because it is work. Our problem is not a lack of intelligence or a lack of passion. Our problem is that we are lazy.

R. C. SPROUL
PROFESSOR OF THEOLOGY AND CHAIRMAN OF
LIGONIER MINISTRIES

We have grasped the mystery of the atom and rejected the sermon on the mount.

OMAR BRADLEY (1893-1981)
FIVE-STAR GENERAL IN THE U.S. ARMY
(COMMENTING IN 1948)

So it must be with today's evangelicals. Following in the steps of Wilberforce, we must confront the moral horrors of our day. And when we work for causes that people across the political spectrum understand as promoting the human good, we break out of the stereotypical "Bible-thumping bigot" mold.

CHARLES W. COLSON
FORMER WHITE HOUSE COUNSEL AND FOUNDER OF
PRISON FELLOWSHIP
CHRISTIANITY TODAY, FEBRUARY 2004

I have sometimes seen more in a line of the Bible than I could well tell how to stand under; and yet at another time the whole Bible hath been to me as dry as a stick.

JOHN BUNYAN (1628–1688)
ENGLISH WRITER AND NONCONFORMIST PREACHER
GRACE ABOUNDING

The Bible is the world's best-selling book as well as the world's most shoplifted book!

JERRY MACGREGOR AND MARIE PRYS
*1001 SURPRISING THINGS YOU SHOULD KNOW ABOUT
CHRISTIANITY*, 2002

Last eve I passed beside a blacksmith's door,
And heard the anvil ring the vesper chime;
Then, looking in, I saw upon the floor
Old hammers, worn with beating years of time.

"How many anvils have you had," said I,
"To wear and batter all these hammers so?"
"Just one," said he, with twinkling eye,
"The anvil wears the hammers out, you know."

And so, thought I, the anvil of God's Word,
For ages skeptic blows have beat upon;
Yet, though the noise of falling blows was heard,
The anvil is unharmed, the hammers gone.

AUTHOR UNKNOWN
"THE ANVIL–GOD'S WORD"

The Bible is like a telescope. If a man looks *through* his telescope, then he sees worlds beyond; but if he looks *at* his telescope, then he does not see anything but that. The Bible is a thing to be looked through, to see that which is beyond; but most people only look at it; and so they see only the dead letter.

PHILLIPS BROOKS (1835–1893)
BISHOP OF MASSACHUSETTS

Once upon a time, the Bible was a big black book with golden-edged pages that required a course in body-building before you could lift it off the shelf. In recent times, though, the Bible's been repackaged and has sunsets and puppy dogs and other marketing-friendly pictures on the cover, and no longer weighs a ton. But even though now it looks like any other bestseller, the Bible still stands out as being a book unlike any other.

SIMON JENKINS
THE BIBLE FROM SCRATCH, 2004

In the nineteenth century there was much discussion in Britain about whether the Bible should be studied "like any other book." There were those who argued against doing this, fearful of what the outcome would be. They lost the argument and the Bible showed that it could more than stand up to the most searching and detailed scrutiny that any text, let alone a religious text, has ever been subjected.

THE OXFORD ILLUSTRATED HISTORY OF THE BIBLE, 2001

It is essential . . . to remember that the Bible is a book of principles, and not a book of disjointed aphorisms. Isolated texts may often be made to sanction things to which the principles of Scripture are totally opposed. I believe all fanaticism comes in this way.

HANNAH WHITALL SMITH (1832–1911)
QUAKER EVANGELIST
THE CHRISTIAN'S SECRET OF A HAPPY LIFE, 1870

It is a fallacy to suppose that by omitting a subject you teach nothing about it. On the contrary, you teach that it is to be omitted, and that it is therefore a matter of secondary importance.

SIR WALTER H. MOBERLY (1881–1974)
ViCE-CHANCELLOR OF OXFORD UNIVERSITY
(ON THE BIBLE IN THE CURRICULUM)

It's just called "The Bible" now. We dropped the word "Holy" to give it a more mass-market appeal.

EDITOR AT HODDER & STOUGHTON PUBLISHERS
(QUOTED IN THE *DAILY TELEGRAPH*, LONDON, 1989)

Be careful how you live, you may be the only Bible some person ever reads.

W. J. TOMS
DETROIT NEWS

Those who talk of the Bible as a "monument of English prose" are merely admiring it as a monument over the grave of Christianity.

T. S. ELIOT (THOMAS STEARNS ELIOT) (1888–1965)
ANGLO-AMERICAN POET, CRITIC AND DRAMATIST
RELIGION AND LITERATURE, 1935

Where is the blessedness I knew
When first I saw the Lord?
Where is the soul-refreshing view
Of Jesus and his word?

What peaceful hours I once enjoyed!
How sweet their memory still!
But they have left an aching void
The world can never fill.

WILLIAM COWPER (1731–1800)
ENGLISH POET, HYMN WRITER AND TRANSLATOR
"WALKING WITH GOD"

The Church is not in the business of maintaining buildings; we're in the job for promoting the values of Christ and the gospel.

GEORGE CAREY
ARCHBISHOP OF CANTERBURY

Holy Scripture is so sublime that there is no one in the world wise enough, not even anyone with learning and spirit, who would not find it totally beyond their capacity to understand Scripture fully; still, they babble something about it.

ANGELA OF FOLGINO (1248–1309)
ITALIAN MYSTIC

Though our covetous clerics are altogether carried away by bribery, heresy, and many other sins, and though they despise and oppose the scripture, as much as they can, yet the common people cry out for the scripture, to know it, and obey it, with great cost and peril to their lives.

PROLOGUE TO THE WYCLIF BIBLE, c.1395

The only protection from our own pride, fear, ignorance and impatience as we study the Bible is fellowship with the living Word, the Lord himself, invoked in constant supplication from the midst of his people.

DALLAS WILLARD
SOUTHERN BAPTIST MINISTER, THEOLOGIAN AND SCHOLAR
HEARING GOD, 1999

Wherever we see the Word of God purely preached and heard, there a church of God exists, even if it swarms with many faults.

JOHN CALVIN (1509-1564)
FRENCH-BORN REFORMATION THEOLOGIAN

So far as I can remember, there is not one word in the Gospels in praise of intelligence.

BERTRAND RUSSELL (1872-1970)
ENGLISH PHILOSOPHER AND MATHEMATICIAN

Darwin's thesis regarding the evolutionary origin of the species through a prolonged series of separations was the final bombshell that altered forever the traditional assumption that science and biblical testimony could sit comfortable side by side.

THE OXFORD ILLUSTRATED HISTORY OF THE BIBLE, 2001

While thousands, careless of the damning sin, Kiss the Book's outside who ne'er look within.

WILLIAM COWPER (1731-1800)
ENGLISH POET, HYMN WRITER AND TRANSLATOR
"EXPOSTULATION"

The rivers of America will run with blood filled to
their banks before we will submit to them taking
the Bible out of our schools.

BILLY SUNDAY (WILLIAM A. SUNDAY) (1862–1935)
AMERICAN EVANGELIST

How can the church become a Scripture-based
community, even where it earnestly longs to do so?
Those who can naively affirm the bumper-sticker
slogan, "God said it, I believe it, that settles it," are
oblivious to the question-begging inherent in the
formulation: there is no escape from the imperative
of interpreting the Word. Bumper-sticker
hermeneutics will not do.

RICHARD B. HAYS
AMERICAN THEOLOGIAN AND ETHICIST
THE MORAL VISION OF THE NEW TESTAMENT, 1996

I have spent a lot of time searching through the Bible
for loop-holes.

W. C. FIELDS (WILLIAM CLAUDE DUKENFIELD)
(1879–1946)
AMERICAN ENTERTAINER
(REMARK DURING HIS LAST ILLNESS)

Nature does not go forth in search of Christianity; but Christianity goes forth to knock at the door of nature and, if possible, awaken her out of her sluggishness. . . . And seeing, that the disinclination of the human heart to entertain the overtures of the gospel, forms a mightier obstacle to its reception among men than all the oceans and continents which missionaries have to traverse, there ought to be a series of aggressive measures in behalf of Christianity, carried on from one age to another, in every clime and country of Christendom.

THOMAS CHALMERS (1780–1847)
SCOTTISH EVANGELIST AND ORATOR

Most people are bothered by those passages in Scripture which they cannot understand; but as for me, I always noticed that the passages in Scripture which trouble me most are those which I do understand.

MARK TWAIN (SAMUEL LANGHORNE CLEMENS)
(1835–1910)
AMERICAN WRITER AND HUMORIST

The revelation of God . . . is not to be equated with a book, but it comes to us only through the medium of that book and, when the book is no longer read and understood by Christians, they have been cut off decisively from the roots of their distinctively Christian existence.

JAMES D. SMART
THE STRANGE SILENCE OF THE BIBLE IN THE CHURCH, 1970

Philosophical argument has sometimes shaken my reason for the faith that was in me; but my heart has always assured me that the gospel of Jesus Christ must be reality.

DANIEL WEBSTER (1782–1852)
AMERICAN STATESMAN, LAWYER AND ORATOR

It is a strange thing that the Bible is so little read. I am reading it regularly through at present. I dare say there are many people of distinction in London who know nothing about it.

JAMES BOSWELL (1740–1795)
BRITISH AUTHOR AND BIOGRAPHER OF
DR. SAMUEL JOHNSON

As any high-school or college teacher will testify, allusions to even the most celebrated Biblical texts now draw a blank. One is, indeed, tempted to define modernism in Western culture in terms of the recession of the Old and New Testaments from the common currency of recognition. . . . The King James Bible and the Luther Bible provided much of our civilization with its alphabet or referential immediacy, not only in the spheres of personal and public piety but in those of politics, social institutions, and the life of the literary and aesthetic imagination.

GEORGE STEINER
LITERARY CRITIC
"THE GOOD BOOKS," *THE NEW YORKER*, JANUARY 1988

Why do I forget God's Word? . . . To forget is not only a matter of the mind but also of the whole person, including the heart. That on which my life and soul depend I cannot forget. The more I begin to love the ordinances of God in creation and in his Word, the more they will be present for me at every hour. Only love guards against forgetting.

DIETRICH BONHOEFFER (1905-1945)
GERMAN LUTHERAN PASTOR AND THEOLOGIAN
(IMPRISONED AND EXECUTED BY THE NAZIS)

Every type of destruction that human philosophy, human science, human reason, human art, human cunning, human force, and human brutality could bring to bear against a book has been brought to bear against this Book, and yet the Bible stands absolutely unshaken today. At times almost all the wise and great of the earth have been pitted against the Bible, and only an obscure few for it.

Yet it has stood.

REUBEN ARCHER TORREY (1856-1928)
AMERICAN EVANGELIST, EDUCATOR AND WRITER

The Bible—banned, burned, beloved. More widely read, more frequently attacked than any other book in history. Generations of intellectuals have attempted to discredit it; dictators of every age have outlawed it and executed those who read it. Yet soldiers carry it into battle believing it more powerful than their weapons. Fragments of it smuggled into solitary prison cells have transformed ruthless killers into gentle saints.

CHARLES W. COLSON
FORMER WHITE HOUSE COUNSEL AND FOUNDER OF
PRISON FELLOWSHIP

We may observe that the teaching of Our Lord Himself, in which there is no imperfection, is not given us in that cut-and-dried, fool-proof, systematic fashion we might have expected or desired. He wrote no book. We have only reported sayings, most of them uttered in answer to questions, shaped in some degree by their context. . . .

Since this is what God has done, this, we must conclude, was best. It may be that what we should have liked would have been fatal to us if granted. It may be indispensable that Our Lord's teaching, by that elusiveness (to our systematising intellect), should demand a response from the whole man, should make it so clear that there is no question of learning a subject but of steeping ourselves in a Personality, acquiring a new outlook and temper, breathing a new atmosphere, suffering Him, in His own way, to rebuild in us the defaced image of Himself.

C. S. LEWIS (CLIVE STAPLES LEWIS) (1898-1963)
IRISH LITERARY SCHOLAR, CHRISTIAN APOLOGIST
AND WRITER
REFLECTIONS ON THE PSALMS, 1955

My *apologia* is an argument in favor of taking the Bible seriously, and it is addressed in part at least to those who either trivialize it or idolize it, and who thereby miss its dynamic, living and transforming quality. It is an argument addressed as well to those who are in search of spiritual and moral grounding in their chaotic lives, and who may have heard of the Bible but know little and want to know more. It is also an argument that condemns the lazy, simpleminded approach that many are tempted to take when considering the serious matter of Bible interpretation. Finally, it is also an invitation to enter into the Bible and let it enter into us, all of us, and most particularly into those who have been excluded from the faith of the Bible by the use of the Bible.

PETER J. GOMES
PREACHER AT HARVARD UNIVERSITY
*THE GOOD BOOK: READING THE BIBLE WITH MIND
AND HEART,* 1996

I am distressed that our princes take the Word of God no more seriously than a cow does a game of chess.

ARGULA VON GRUMBACH (C.1492–1563)
BAVARIAN SUPPORTER OF THE REFORMATION

The Bible has furnished, and still furnishes, the basic, most fundamental building blocks of Western civilization. Therefore, this is true: If you live in this civilization and don't have a fair knowledge of the Bible, you are *basically uneducated.* You may know a lot of things, but you won't have the foggiest notion of where all these things came from, what they all mean, how they are interrelated, what to use them for, and generally what makes them tick.

ROBERT L. SHORT
THE BIBLE ACCORDING TO PEANUTS, 1990

The deathless Book has survived three great dangers: the negligence of its friends; the false systems built upon it; the warfare of those who have hated it.

ISAAC TAYLOR (1787–1865)
ENGLISH POLITICAL AND RELIGIOUS WRITER

The Bible is to us what the star was to the wise men; but if we spend all our time in gazing upon it, observing its motions, and admiring its splendor, without being led to Christ by it, the use of it will be lost to us.

THOMAS ADAMS (1871–1940)
ENGLISH ARCHITECT AND TOWN PLANNER

The science of this world, which has become a great
power, has, especially in the last century, analyzed
everything divine handed down to us in the old
books. After this cruel analysis the learned of the
world have nothing left of all that was sacred of old.
But they have only analyzed the parts and overlooked
the whole, and indeed their blindness is marvelous.
Yet the whole still stands steadfastly before their
eyes, and the gates of hell shall not prevail against it.
Has it not lasted nineteen centuries, is it not still a
living, a moving power in the individual soul and in
the masses of people? It is still as strong and living
even in the souls of atheists, who have destroyed
everything! For even those who have renounced
Christianity and attack it, in their inmost being still
follow the Christian ideal, for hitherto neither their
subtlety nor the ardor of their hearts has been able to
create a higher ideal of man and of virtue than the
ideal given by Christ of old.

FYODOR DOSTOEVSKY (1821–1881)
RUSSIAN NOVELIST
THE BROTHERS KARAMAZOV, 1879

His books well trimm'd and in the gayest style,
Like regimental coxcombs rank and file,
Adorn his intellects as well as shelves
And teach him notions splendid as themselves.
The Bible only stands neglected there,
Though that of all most worthy of his care,
And, like an infant troublesome awake,
Is left to sleep for peace and quiet sake.

WILLIAM COWPER (1731–1800)
ENGLISH POET, HYMN WRITER AND TRANSLATOR
"TRUTH"

Because of lack of fortitude and faithfulness on the
part of God's people, God's Word has many times
been allowed to be bent, to conform to the
surrounding, passing, changing culture of that
moment rather than to stand as the inerrant Word of
God judging the form of the world spirit and the
surrounding culture of that moment.

FRANCIS A. SCHAEFFER (1912–1984)
AMERICAN PRESBYTERIAN MINISTER AND SPEAKER

Alas, how much time I have lost and wasted, which, had I been wise, I should have devoted to reading and studying the Bible! But my evil heart obstructs the dictates of my judgment, I often feel a reluctance to read this book of books . . . while the fountain of living waters are close within my reach.

JOHN NEWTON (1725–1807)
EVANGELICAL HYMN WRITER AND FORMER SLAVE TRADER

Heaven and earth will pass away, but my words will never pass away.

MATTHEW 24:35

GUIDE TO THEMES

The following indicative themes provide a guide for identifying quotations within each chapter.

THE POWER OF THE BIBLE TO ENCOURAGE FAITH
Belief, Conversion, Devotion, Grace, Heart, Holy Spirit, Hope, Love of God, Nurture, Prayer, Revelation, Salvation, Soul, Spiritual Life, Transformation, Worship

THE POWER OF THE BIBLE TO PROVIDE INSTRUCTION
Answers, Application of Scripture, Commentary, Direction, Duty, Education, Ethics, Guidance, Knowledge, Learning, Message, Obedience, Purpose, Reformation, Study, Understanding, Will of God, Wisdom

THE POWER OF THE BIBLE TO ILLUMINATE CHRIST
Fulfillment, Gift, Gospel, Image of Christ, King, Knowledge of Jesus, Living Word, Perfection, Revelation, Sacrifice, Salvation, Son of God, Teacher, The Cross, Victor, Vision of Jesus, Work of Christ

THE POWER OF THE BIBLE TO REVEAL TRUTH
Authority, Authors, Comfort, Conviction, Correction, Discernment, Discovery, Freedom, Infallibility, Inspiration, Light, Promises, Proof, Recognition, Record, Relevance, Reliability

THE POWER OF THE BIBLE TO INSPIRE THE IMAGINATION

Art, Beauty, Creativity, Culture, Drama, Dreams, Entertainment, Excellence, Film, Language, Literature, Masterpiece, Music, Mystery, Nature, Newness, Poetry, Story, Vibrancy

THE POWER OF THE BIBLE TO SHAPE CIVILIZATIONS

Citizenship, Civic Virtue, Dissemination of Bible, Evangelization, Government, History, Humanity, Justice, Law, Leadership, Liberty, Missions, National Prosperity, Oratory, Politics, Power, Public Good, Social Movements, War

THE POWER OF THE BIBLE TO ENDURE CHALLENGES

Biblical Criticism, Confusion, Disregard, Heresy, Humanism, Hypocrisy, Intellectualism, Laziness, Misuse, Science, Sin, Tyranny, Warfare, Worldliness

SELECTED BIBLIOGRAPHY

$\mathcal{M}$any of the quotations in this collection have already referenced the full author's name, book title, and date of publication. In addition, the author wishes to acknowledge the following secondary sources.

12,000 Inspirational Quotations: A Treasury of Spiritual Insights and Practical Wisdom, edited by Frank S. Mead. Springfield, Mass: Federal Street Press, 2000 (originally published 1965).

12,000 Religious Quotations, edited by Frank S. Mead. Grand Rapids, Mich.: Baker Book House, 1989.

Barnes & Noble Book of Quotations, edited by Robert I. Fitzhenry. New York: Harper & Row Publishers, 1987.

Bartlett's Familiar Quotations, edited by Emily Morrison Beck. Boston: Little, Brown and Company, 15th edition, 1980.

The Believer's Daily Renewal, by Andrew Murray. Minneapolis: Bethany House Publishers, 2004.

The Best-Loved Poems of the American People, selected by Hazel Felleman. New York: Doubleday, 1936.

Bible Promises for Mom. Nashville, Tenn.: Broadman & Holman Publishers, 2003.

Biblical Quotations: A Reference Guide, edited by Martin H. Manser.

New York: Facts on File, Inc., 2001.

The Book of Positive Quotations, compiled by John Cook. Minneapolis: Fairview Press, 1993.

Cambridge Illustrated History of Religions, edited by John Bowker. Cambridge: Cambridge University Press, 2002.

The Christian Quote Book, compiled by Rachel Quillin. Uhrichsville, Ohio: Barbour Publishing, 2004.

The Christian Theology Reader, edited by Alister E. McGrath. Oxford: Blackwell, 2nd edition, 2001.

The Columbia World of Quotations, edited by Robert Andrews, Mary Biggs and Michael Seidel. New York: Columbia University Press, 1996.

A Concise Lincoln Dictionary: Thoughts and Statements, compiled by Ralph B. Winn. New York: Philosophical Library, 1959.

A Dictionary of Quotations, edited by Philip H. Dalbiac. London: Thomas Nelson and Sons, Ltd. (undated).

Dictionary of Religious Quotations, compiled by William Neil. London: Mowbrays, 1975.

Disciplines for the Inner Life, by Bob Benson, Sr. and Michael W. Benson. Nashville: Thomas Nelson, 1989.

The Doubleday Prayer Collection, selected by Mary Batchelor. New York: Doubleday, 1997. (Originally published in England as *The Lion Prayer Collection*, 1992)

The Doubleday Christian Quotation Collection, compiled by Hannah Ward and Jennifer Wild. New York: Doubleday, 1998. (Originally published in England as *The Lion Christian Quotation Collection*, 1997)

Encarta Book of Quotations, edited by Bill Swainson. New York: St. Martin's Press, 2000.

An Encyclopedia of Compelling Quotations, compiled by R. Daniel Watkins. Peabody, Mass.: Hendrickson Publishers, 2001.

Fill Me With Hope: Classic Christian Writings, compiled by Paul M. Miller. Uhrichsville, Ohio: Barbour Publishing, 2004.

Glimpses of the Divine, by Bishop Cyril Bulley. Worthing, Sussex: Churchman Publishing Ltd., 1987.

Good News for the World: The Story of the Bible Society, by Roger Steer. Oxford: Monarch Books, 2004.

The Great Thoughts, compiled by George Seldes. New York: Ballantine Books, 1985.

Great Treasury of Western Thought, edited by Mortimer J. Adler and Charles Van Doren. New York: R. R. Bowker Company, 1977.

Halley's Bible Handbook: An Abbreviated Bible Commentary. Grand Rapids, Mich.: Zondervan, 24th edition, 1965.

Harper's Bible Commentary, edited by James L. Mays. San Francisco: Harper & Row Publishers, 1988.

The Home Book of American Quotations, selected by Bruce Bohl. New York: Dodd, Mead & Company, 1967.

The Home Book of Quotations Classical and Modern, selected by Burton Stevenson. New York: Dodd, Mead & Company, 10th edition, 1967.

Hoyt's New Cyclopedia of Practical Quotations, compiled by Kate Louis Roberts. New York: Funk & Wagnall's, 1940.

The Hymnal for Worship and Celebration. Waco, Texas: Word Music, 1986.

In His Presence: Daily Devotionals through the Gospel of Matthew, edited by Lance Wubbels. Lynnwood, Wash.: Emerald Books, 1998.

In the Beginning: The Story of the King James Bible, by Alister McGrath. London: Hodder & Stoughton, 2001.

The International Dictionary of Thoughts, compiled by P. Bradley, Leo F. Daniels and Thomas C. Jones. Chicago: J. G. Ferguson Publishing Co., 1969.

The International Thesaurus of Quotations, compiled by Rhoda Thomas Tripp. New York: Thomas Y. Crowell Company, 1970.

The Journey Inward: Quotations for the Soul, by Rosalie Maggio. New York: Barnes & Noble Books, 2001.

The Making of the English Bible, by Benson Bobrick. London: Weidenfeld & Nicolson, 2001.

Morrow's International Dictionary of Contemporary Quotations, compiled by Jonathon Green. New York: William Morrow and Company, 1982.

The New Encyclopedia of Christian Quotations, compiled by Mark Water. Alresford, Hampshire: John Hunt Publishing Ltd., 2000.

The New International Dictionary of Quotations, selected by Margaret Miner and Hugh Rawson. Harmondsworth: Penguin Books, 3rd edition, 2000.

The New Oxford Book of Christian Verse, edited by Donald Davie. Oxford: Oxford University Press, 1981.

The Oxford Book of Prayer, edited by George Appleton. Oxford: Oxford University Press, 1985.

The Oxford Dictionary of Modern Quotations, edited by Tony Augarde. Oxford: Oxford University Press, 1991.

The Oxford Dictionary of Quotations, edited by Elizabeth Knowles. Oxford: Oxford University Press, 5th edition, 1999.

The Oxford Illustrated History of the Bible, edited by John Rogerson. Oxford: Oxford University Press, 2001.

Peter's Quotations: Ideas for Our Time, edited by Laurence J. Peter. New York: William Morrow & Company, 1977.

Practical Christianity. Carmel, N.Y.: Guideposts, 1987.

The Quotable Woman: The First 5,000 Years, edited by Elaine Patrow. New York: Checkmark Books, 2001.

Quotations of Courage and Vision, compiled by Carl Hermann Voss. New York: Association Press, 1972.

Religious & Spiritual Quotations, edited by Geoffrey Parrinder. London: Routledge, 1990.

Simpson's Contemporary Quotations, compiled by James B. Simpson. Boston: Houghton Mifflin, 1988.

Spiritual Companions: An Introduction to the Christian Classics, by Peter Toon. London: Marshall Pickering, 1990.

Teachings of the Christian Mystics, edited by Andrew Harvey. Boston: Shambala Publications Inc., 1998.

The Times Book of Quotations. Glasgow: Times Books, HarperCollins Publishers, 2000.

Topical Encyclopedia of Living Quotations, edited by Sherwood Eliot Wirt and Kersten Beckstrom. Minneapolis: Bethany House Publishers, 1982.

Watch and Pray: Christian Teachings on the Practice of Prayer, by Lorraine Kisly. New York: Bell Tower, 2002.

The Westminster Collection of Christian Quotations, compiled by Martin H. Manser. Louisville: Westminster John Knox Press, 2001.

Wisdom for Christian Living, by Matthew Henry. Uhrichsville, Ohio: Barbour Publishing, 2003.

A Woman's Treasury of Faith, Grand Rapids, Mich.: Family Christian Press, 2004.

A Woman's Treasury of Grace, Grand Rapids, Mich.: Family Christian Press, 2004.

INDEX OF SOURCES

*From *The New International Version* unless otherwise identified.

HYMNS, SONGS AND
POEMS *(BY TITLE)*

DEAR READERS,

Do you have a favorite quotation about the Bible? Perhaps a special thought caught your attention while reading the newspaper or studying a devotional text or listening to a sermon. I would be delighted to hear from you. Please send the full quotation, author, date and other reference information to:

Dr. Isabella D. Bunn
% Bethany House Publishers
Editorial Department
11400 Hampshire Avenue South
Bloomington, Minnesota 55438

Or send an e-mail to: *editorial@bethanyhouse.com*

As you have seen, the entries in this volume are drawn from a wide range of characters, time periods, and perspectives. But they represent just a fraction of the world's most powerful observations about the world's most powerful book. We at Bethany House Publishers would be privileged to consider your contributions—from the famous and not-so-famous—as we prepare another collection of surprising quotes about the Bible!

With thanks and best regards,
Isabella